THE BIGCHILL

SUMMER LIVING

Edited by Phil Daoust and Bibi van der Zee

contents

the origins of the festival

by mr.scruff

many years ago, having a cup of tea in the countryside involved a lot of work

one's butler would have to load a carriage with all the required equipment

tables, chairs...

extra butlers...

portable stove..

kettle..

fine china..

biscuits, exquisite cakes..

& a spare horse .

the invention of the camping stove & flask put many butlers out of work, and meant that tea in the country was now a much easier & affordable option

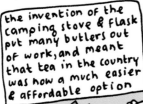

this activity rapidly gained popularity

until nearly every field was constantly full of people drinking tea from a flask

one bright spark thought that it would be nice to entertain the crowds of tea drinkers with music & other attractions

of course, the tea drinkers loved this feature, and these events started to appear all over the place

originally, they were called...

flask enthusiasts sipping tea in various attractive locations

but this was eventually simplified to 'festival', a name that still exists to this day!

cheers

foreword

The word 'chill' became widespread in the 1980s and 1990s as a slang term meaning to calm down. Not surprisingly perhaps, its first recorded use in this context was in the 1970s. It comes from what is rather stiffly known as Black English slang, which has frequently been a source of informal words adopted into what is known even more stiffly as Standard English, often through the medium of musical styles originating in America, such as rap and hip-hop.

This is hardly the first incarnation of 'chill' as a slang term. An older meaning, first recorded in the 1870s, was to lose interest in something. Since the late 1920s, 'chill' has also been used to mean to quash and even to kill. The new meaning, however, is a fine example of the English habit of using words relating to heat and cold to describe emotions. 'Cool' has referred to calmness since Old English times; 'chill' is simply an extension of the metaphor. And the evolution continues: the new sense of 'chilling' has recently been extended to mean to relax among friends.

Whatever. 'Chill' is a wonderful example of how languages change in ways that are at once unpredictable and entirely comprehensible. In fact, being unpredictable and at the same time entirely comprehensible goes a long way towards summing up the Big Chill festival. You'll find out all about that in this book, which celebrates the independent spirit of the UK festival scene.

This book also aims to be an almanac of summer ideas for the British Person Who Summers, with a particularly, peculiarly festivally bent. Now more than ever, the British summer is, among many other wonderful things such as a lightness of heart and thinness of jumper, all about festivals. That might mean listening to some of the world's greatest musicians, exploring the gravity of West Country ales, zipping yourself into a sleeping bag for a human snail race, or even dressing up as a Guantanamo Bay detainee – a major fancy dress trend in 2008's summer festivals. Reinterpreting the things that freak us out in normal life is an element of festival catharsis, and, contentiously, part of the fun.

I've been given the job of getting people together to celebrate and encourage a side of life called pleasure, and it's a huge privilege. I hope this book will help you to share it.

Katrina Larkin, co-founder of the Big Chill festival

Introduct

Music festivals were once regarded as public enemy number one, plunging society into an abyss of drugs, free love and unwashed hair. At Woodstock in 1969, as the New York Times reported how tens of thousands of 'youths' were getting 'stoned' on 'grass', one American cop complained they couldn't all be 'busted' because there simply weren't enough jails. In 1970, after 600,000 hippies invaded the Isle of Wight, the festival's own promoter described it as a monster that had got out of control. The following year, parliament passed a law to ban even tiny gatherings on the island. How the 'squares' must have cheered ...

And yet festivals have not just survived but flourished. In Britain, where you're as likely to contract trench foot in the summer as you are sunburn, giant open-air parties nonetheless spring up every year from Somerset in the West Country to Loch Ness in the Highlands. Whatever your mood or musical tastes, you'll find an event to suit you, from the relaxed and family-friendly Big Chill in the gorgeous grounds of Eastnor Castle to Deathfest in slightly less idyllic Leeds. Most offer a dazzling range of non-musical attractions: cocktails, comedy, circuses, cowboys ... You don't even have to rough it under canvas: at the seaside town of Minehead, All Tomorrow's Parties will put you up in Butlin's.

Whether this is your first or your 40th festival, this book aims to guide you through the possibilities. For May, June, July, August and September, Guardian writers highlight the month's most exciting festival, and explain what sets it apart from the rest, and how to make the most of it. If you like the location so much that you want to extend your stay (or simply want to escape the hurly-burly of the main event for a few hours) we've also provided a detailed list of local amenities, such as campsites, pubs and open-air swimming spots.

Is your first choice sold out? Or have you had such a great time that you want to get the tent out again as soon as possible? Don't worry: we've included monthly listings of other festivals. And we've interviewed a handful of the colourful characters you might bump into, from stilt-walker Rachel Hyde to Jerry Morgan, proud proprietor of a solar-powered cinema. Do say hello if you recognise them: it'll make a nice change from everyone gawping at Kate Moss.

But as the title suggests, there's more to this Big Chill Guide to Summer Living than festivals alone. If you fancy a week in the countryside or simply want to make the most of a cloudless afternoon, each month has a helpful directory of non-

festival activities, ranging from ghost-hunting in York to naked gardening in your own back yard. If you're planning a night or two under canvas, we also explain some easy ways to increase your comfort (such as pitching a tent) or unwind or impress your friends (like identifying the constellations).

In the mood for a little silliness? We've got games for anywhere between two and 20 players. If all that leaves you needing a pick-me-up, there are drinks recipes from the Big Chill bar staff and food recipes from some of its most popular suppliers.

And if this summer turns out to be more chilly than chilled? Don't worry: on page 24 we tell you how to build a campfire.

Phil Daoust

may

'A slice of English paradise'
– Stewart Edwards

illustration Ryan Miglinczy, www.yetivsyeti.co.uk

All Tomo Parties

Somerset

www.atpfestival.com

In 1966 when the Velvet Underground wrote their doomy song about the nightlife of the future, they probably weren't thinking about a fun-filled festival set in a holiday camp. When Nico sang about poor girls in hand-me-down dresses, she probably didn't visualise them joining boys in charity-shop shirts, heading down to the north Somerset coast to enjoy three days of music.

Since 2007, however, the All Tomorrow's Parties organisation, or ATP, has been running three-day festivals in the Butlins holiday camp in Minehead. ATP formed in 1999 launching an annual festival at the Pontin's venue in Camber Sands, Sussex. As the ATP brand grew in popularity over the years, with its programme of album performances and own record label, it became time to find a bigger site, so the team headed west.

Now, 57,000 people attend each of the two ATP weekends in May, and both offer a strangely lovely start to the festival season. After all, Minehead is better known for its coastal walks and teashops than for bearded men in band T-shirts circling the corner shops for cigarettes and booze. Then there's the holiday camp itself. With its big tents, down-at-heel pubs and carpeted bars, it is usually a hub

So what were you expecting at a seaside festival ... mud?

for hen weekends, reunited friends and holiday-making families, not folks who like Autechre more than Abba.

But somehow these very different worlds go well together. After all, Butlins feels like a staging post from a bygone time, and so does this festival. ATP harks back to the intimate, non-corporate roots of the original festival experience, and by showcasing alternative music in the old-fashioned sense – before gel-haired, chart-bothering bands made the term theirs – ATP clearly has different values. The ATP team prizes artists who value experimentation and waywardness, and has hosted musicians from legendary figures to up-and-coming mavericks.

ATP also has a policy of appointing curators, which gives every weekend its distinct personality. These have included big guns like Portishead, cult concerns like Dirty Three, and art-world provocateurs like Jake and Dinos Chapman. For 2009, ATP has decided to give their first weekend over to the fans, and the second to American band the Breeders.

Music is king at ATP, with the bands and DJs playing on until the early hours. Still, there are other weird and wonderful ways to waste one's time. The best is the Butlins Splash Waterworld, with its wave pool and flumes. It's a good place to see skinny limbs and retro bathing suits, but get there early to beat the crowds for the raft ride. Elsewhere, there is the 10-pin bowling alley, the amusement arcade and

page 16 ▶

THE BiGCHill recommends

The Great Escape

Brighton www.escapegreat.com

No mud, no burgers, no 60-strong queue for the cashpoint ... call this a festival? In fact Brighton's Great Escape is more of a conference, or an industry showcase – a shindig at a push. It was started by veteran band booker Martin Elbourne with the aim of letting A&R people and other industry types sample more than 300 bands in the space of three days, in venues all across Brighton and Hove. 'We are trying to provide a platform for export-ready international acts and give them the opportunity to showcase in front of the UK and international music industry,' said the event booker, Olly Hodgson, in 2008. Party on, Olly.

But it's not quite as corporate as that makes it sound. Hardcore music fans love the Great Escape for the sheer number and variety of performances – almost as much as locals love it for the chance it gives them to see huge names such as Bon Iver without venturing any further than the end of their road. Make no mistake: the names really are big. The Fratellis and the Gossip got their breakthroughs here in 2006, future performers include Kasabian, Little Boots and Metronomy, plus countless (possibly) rising stars such as Future of the Left, the Vivian Girls and We Were Promised Jetpacks. They play in pubs, they play in clubs; they even play in people's front rooms and webcast the performance. Festival-goers should be warned that sets are short, often less than an hour, and queues to get into the hotter shows can be painful. Still, the small size of many of the venues means that gigs can be startlingly intimate, with none of the usual barriers between musicians and audience.

There's another dimension to the weekend, too. In time-honoured conference style, the days are filled with panels, discussions, debates about anything and everything to do with the industry; anyone with a delegate ticket (£120) can attend these and catch pearls of wisdom dropped by such luminaries as Jon Savage, Jah Wobble, Pete Jenner, John Leckie and the Guardian's own Alexis Petridis. Gig-only tickets are an incredibly reasonable £39.50 for a three-day pass, at the early bird price. An extra 10 quid gets you into the 'artists' village'. But if you really want to talk to some foxy lead singer, chances are you might see him or her doing the rounds of Brighton's pubs a little later on – it's that kind of a festival.

Carrie O'Grady

the big-screen cinema, and there are enough fast-food outlets to add bulk to the whip-thin. If festival-goers venture outside, they will find the sand and sea at the gate, and steam train rides on the West Somerset Railway 10 minutes away.

But let's not forget the real cherry on the ATP cake: the Butlins chalet accommodation. This is a boon for the ageing indie fan or those terminally shy of tent poles. Whatever the weather, attendees can put traumatic memories of chemical toilets and sleeping bags behind them, and crash out in a bed in their own room with a bathroom, or a self-catering set with friends. Kitchens in the self-catering accommodation also mean festival-goers can even eat before going out. And, for those hungover mornings and idle moments in the musical lineup, there is even a TV with an ATP channel which shows artfully chosen programmes and films.

All in all, ATP is a festival that is civilised and intimate when it needs to be, and uncivilised and alternative-spirited when it doesn't. Bring food, swimming trunks, and well-prepared eardrums to have a good time, and make sure to leave your musical inhibitions, as well as your razor, at home. Follow these rules and when Monday comes around, unlike the Velvet Underground and Nico, none will go mourning.

Jude Rogers

Sticking around

Minehead and South Somerset/Exmoor

Now that the festival season is off to a good start, perhaps you should treat yourself to a few more days out of the office. You'll need your strength for a busy summer.

WHERE TO CAMP

If you're suffering from seaside holiday camp overkill and need a change of scenery, just inland from Minehead is a beautiful and secluded campsite on the banks of the river Exe in Exmoor National Park. Westermill Farm has river swimming, home-reared beef, pork and lamb for sale in the shop and you're allowed to make a camp fire. The site also has several Scandanavian-style chalets for rent if you're that way inclined.
www.westermill.com

WHAT TO DO

Walking

Walking in Exmoor National Park, among the gorse and hills, is second to none. There are more than 20 walks to take in the area ranging between 5km-15km.
www.holidayexmoor.co.uk/page20.htm

If you want to make it a walking holiday, you can take the 58km Coleridge Way. Divided into four roughly 15km chunks of varying intensity, the walk can be done in three or four days, camping along the way. Alternatively, pick a section and off you go for the day.
www.coleridgeway.co.uk

There are also guided walks on offer with Richard Medland. He can show you 'his Exmoor' and share his local knowledge.
www.exmoorwalks.co.uk

Swimming

Minehead has a great sandy beach with good facilities or, just along the coast, the seaside town of Lynmouth lies beneath unspoilt wooded hills. Good waves break here so it's popular with surfers.
www.forces-of-nature.co.uk/dbdriven/
beachguide/beachguide.php/
location/70/Lynmouth

Wild spot

Exmoor National Park is habitat to a mixture of wildlife, perhaps owing to the diversity of the terrain. Expect to see nesting coastal birds such as kittiwakes and razorbills while the salt marshes are home to curlews and oystercatchers. Red deer are prevalent across the moors while the woodland is home to red and grey squirrels, and hedgehogs. Perhaps most famous of all is the Exmoor pony – not strictly wild these days, but neither are they domesticated. Don't be deceived by the Exmoor's pint-sized status – the ponies are extremely strong and hardy. You can take a guided trek on one (if you don't weigh more than around 12 stone), and learn about their habitat and conservation in the Exmoor pony centre at Dulverton.
www.exmoorpony.org
www.moorlandmousietrust.org.uk

We dare you

For an exhilarating way to see the unique countryside, take a Barle Valley 4x4 wildlife safari. You can be picked up from Minehead, Dulverston and Dunston and the safaris will take you tracking Exmoor deer and ponies through woods, rivers and fields inaccessible to cars.
www.exmoorwildlifesafaris.co.uk

If it rains

It's a given that a holiday in Britain no matter the duration or time of year will be interrupted by rain so it's handy to have a few indoor activities up your sleeve. Try visiting poet Samuel Taylor Coleridge's house in Exmoor where he lived for many years.
www.nationaltrust.org.uk/main/
w-coleridgecottage

FOOD AND DRINK

Beer

A relatively new microbrewery, Exmoor Ales's reputation is growing fast and the company now produces an impressive selection of award-winning ales.
www.exmoorales.co.uk

Wine

A pioneer of organic production, the Avalon vineyard produces Pennard wines and cider that are made by hand using traditional methods. The vineyard is the only producer of organic mead in the west country and makes raspberry liqueur, as well as elderberry and ginger wine.
www.pennardorganicwines.co.uk

You can also raise a glass at the White Horse, perched by a bridge on the river Exe. You'll find fine food as well as ales at this lovely, family-run pub.
www.exmoor-whitehorse.co.uk

Woodland splendour – Watersmeet in Exmoor National Park

Not for riding ... or for taking home with you. Exmoor's famous ponies.

Local Produce

The Exe Valley Fishery supplies a variety of locally caught smoked fish, plus the opportunity to catch your own.
www.exevalleyfishery.co.uk

You won't go wrong making a stop at Hindon Farm, near Selworthy. Penny and Roger Webber make a mean breakfast with organic local produce and sell their own organic beef, lamb and home-made sausages. There's even accommodation ... with a hot tub.
www.hindonfarm.co.uk

FOR THE KIDS

Learn about traditional falconry using hawks, falcons and eagles. Many of the majestic birds are shown daily in flying displays. Bring your camera. There are also lots of other animals for the kids to see including horses, donkeys and llamas – and cream tea for the adults.
www.exmoorfalconry.co.uk

A beautiful peregrine falcon at the Exmoor Falconry and Animal Farm.

may

Make the most of the month

Party

In an odd, yet somehow pleasing, pairing, May Day is both International Workers' Day and a pagan festival marking the coming of summer and sunshine. As an ancient Irish rhyme puts it, 'Hurray, hurray, the first of May/ F**king outdoors begins today'. In Edinburgh the pagan side is marked every year by the wonderful Beltane fire festival which brings thousands of people to Calton Hill on the night of 30 April. In other parts of the country, May Day has often been marked by demonstrations as activists 'celebrate' with a bit of window-smashing or at least a good dance around the City of London. Every year there's also the traditional London May Day march, with assorted unions joining together to walk through the streets; it's a colourful, larky sort of outing, especially if the sun is shining.
www.beltane.org; www.londonmayday.org

Laugh

You are warned at the beginning of the Bizarre Bath walking tour that you'll learn nothing at all about the city. Instead, JJ and Noel Britten, who have been hosting the walk for over a decade, offer a guide to local sights such as the world's largest bonsai tree, or lead the crowd in a couple of verses of *The Lord Is My Shepherd*.
www.bizarrebath.co.uk

Walk

Most of us like to walk in company: fellow hikers are good talkers, good listeners, and usually understand that sometimes you're out of breath or just want a moment of peace. This makes the Isle of Wight Walking Festival ideal. In 2008, 24,000 people were lured to the event by more than 300 walks catering for all ages and abilities. You can choose from dinosaur walks, speed-dating walks and tours of local gardens or the island's landfill and recycling facilities. You can't really go wrong, as more than half of the island is recognised as an Area of Outstanding Natural Beauty.
www.isleofwightwalkingfestival.co.uk

Paint

Every spring the stylish Glasgow School of Art, housed in Charles Rennie Mackintosh's still surprising building, lays on weekend courses for adults. If you have ever sighed into your pint at the end of an evening about your abandoned artistic ambitions, perhaps this is the answer. Spend a weekend learning 'no fear video editing', bookbinding or painting the human form, with a few evenings out exploring Glasgow's many, many world-class bars. It will either end your creative dream forever, or start a new fire.
www.gsa.ac.uk/gsa.cfm?pid=2604

Read

Ever wanted to see what 40,000 bookworms in a field look like? Head to Hay-on-Wye, the book festival in the Welsh Brecon Beacons about which American playwright Arthur Miller asked, 'Is that some sort of sandwich?' It's been going since the late 70s, and the names get bigger every year. There is invariably one big literary lion mano-a-mano, and most people find time between reading and talking and reading some more to eat and drink quite staggering amounts of food and booze. Take the 'no-book challenge': see if you can go round the town's 36 bookshops as well as attending the debates without buying a single book. Most have found that it can't be done.
www.hayfestival.com/wales

Munch

While Britain slips slowly down some international league tables, there is one area we continue to dominate: British cheese is acknowledged to be right up there with the masters of the world. If you love cheese and want to know more about it, Chris Ashby of AB Cheesemaking is generally acknowledged to be one of the doyennes of the craft. All sorts of luminaries have passed through her doors, and her short courses are regularly booked up, so make sure you reserve your place well in advance.

www.abcheesemaking.co.uk

Glide

There is no feeling in the world to match paragliding. The churning in your stomach just before you take off beneath a flimsy web of nylon and ropes, the sudden absence of earth beneath your feet, the whoosh upwards on a fast-mounting thermal, the world lying opened out before you: it is unforgettable and addictive. Britain has several pockets of expertise and, weather permitting, you can spend a weekend in a Welsh valley or at the base of the Sussex Downs learning the basic safety rules and be up in the air on your own by Sunday afternoon. You'll find all the accredited tutors listed on the British Hang Gliding and Paragliding Association's website: it's all closely regulated, if that makes you feel any safer.

www.bhpa.co.uk

Go ape

Monkey World is one of the world's most high-profile sanctuaries, taking in primates from laboratories and intercepted smuggling rings all over the planet. The animals are brought back to health, then housed in large family groups in big, comfortable enclosures: it's a sanctuary first and a visitor attraction second. That said, people who visit this centre in Dorset help fund the work of the sanctuary and it would not be able to continue otherwise. If you love animals, but find zoos an uncomfortable experience, this may be one version you can live with.

www.monkeyworld.co.uk

Strip

The annual World Naked Gardening Day just doesn't get the coverage it deserves. All anyone ever talks about is the Chelsea Flower Show (which happens later in May), but frankly, it seems like a lot of money and kerfuffle over an activity that should surely be about less fuss and modernity, and more mud and dirt under the fingernails. That's how the organisers of WNGD feel, anyway: they suggest that on the first Saturday in May you 'get naked and do some gardening ... alone, with friends, with family, with your gardening club, or with any other group collected for that purpose. Do it inside your house, in your back yard, on a hiking trail, at a city park, or on the streets. Stay private or go public. Make it a quiet time or make it a public splash.' You could, in theory, be charged with outraging public decency, but this is extremely unlikely – it's more usually reserved for people having sex in public. You will probably just be asked to cover up. If you have ever been even faintly tickled by the idea of naturism, this may be a way to gently dip your toe into the water.

www.wngd.org

Bibi van der Zee

Summer

Building a fire

There can be few outdoor activities quite so relaxing as sitting around an open fire, mesmerised by the dancing flames. It's not enough to throw a few bits of wood together and set light to them, as anyone who has suffered the indignity and frustration of a bonfire that refuses to get going will tell you. Follow these guidelines, however, and in no time you'll be snuggling up with your favourite squeeze while a marshmallow toasts from the end of a stick.

Choosing your site

You can't just go about lighting fires anywhere or the country would burn down in no time. Before starting, check whether open fires are permitted on the land you are on. Even if this is the case, don't light a fire in conditions in which it could get out of control – in strong winds, for example, or in a place where it could set light to combustible material (such as dry vegetation or pine needles). Be careful not to disturb the wildlife – after all, it's their home you're visiting. If you're camping, ensure your fire is downwind of your tent or a stray ember could see your home for the night go up in flames.

Look for somewhere on level ground, out of the wind, and not too far from supplies of dry matter for burning – you don't want to spend your time lugging logs about if you can help it. Avoid trees (and tree roots), grass and cliff faces.

Collecting fuel

The best wood is long dead and as dry as possible. If you're not sure about the suitability of the wood you're collecting, a good rule of thumb is that if it snaps or cracks when you bend it, it's dry. If it feels flexible, the chances are it will not burn. Concentrate on picking up thin pieces that will catch light readily – you can collect larger logs once the fire is established.

Burn, baby, burn ... the perfectly built campfire.

The Big Chill's 'Big Warm' bonfire – don't try this at home.

Laying the fire

Save yourself the bother of arranging a ring of stones. Fires need oxygen to ignite, and all your rock circle will do is block the supply. Instead, create a platform with a row of sticks (about an inch thick) side by side. On top of this base place a generous amount of kindling crisscrossed on top of one another.

Lighting the fire

Tempting though it may be to use a bit of paraffin or petrol to get your fire going, it's in your best interests to resist, since a fire lit like this can be out of control within seconds, taking you with it. Use solid firelighters slipped underneath your kindling or, if you want to get in touch with your inner bushperson, plenty of dry grass, the more fibrous the better.

Keeping it going

Once the fire is lit, don't be tempted to load on huge quantities of wood as this will smother the flames. Instead, add the fuel gradually. A tried and trusted method is to build a pyramid (rather than an unstable tepee). To do this, place two sticks on the base to the left and right of the lit kindling. Place another two sticks across these and nearer the centre, and a further two across them, using thinner sticks as you build four or five storeys.

Cooking

Wait until the flames have died down and carefully place your foil-wrapped food on to (or, in the case of potatoes, snugly down into) the embers. A medium potato (pricked with a fork and wrapped in foil) will take about 45 minutes to cook, so you'll need a good pile of embers to make sure they remain hot for long enough. Boiling a kettle over a fire can be hazardous and time-consuming. Instead, fill a plastic bottle with water (making sure there's absolutely no air in it) and lay it on the fire. The lack of air in the bottle means it won't melt. In three or four minutes (for a half-litre bottle) the water should be hot enough for making tea. It shouldn't work, but it does.

After the fire

Don't forget to clear up. To extinguish the fire, separate the embers and pour water on them. Dispose of them thoughtfully, and cover up the burnt area so that it blends in with the surroundings.

Dixe Wills

Summer

Stargazing

Lying on your back and staring up at a sky festooned with pinpricks of light is another of the joys of a summer evening. There are an estimated 200bn to 400bn stars in our galaxy, and countless others beyond. In the best stargazing conditions – a clear, moonless night and no light pollution – you should be able to see around 750 of them with the naked eye. Climb a mountain and this number rises to about 4,000. However, trying to identify constellations can be a bewildering experience, particularly when none of them seem to bear any resemblance to the flying horses, water snakes and sundry arcane mythical characters to which they owe their names. Add to that the appearance of planets, shooting stars and orbiting satellites and confusion reigns. Here, then, are a few pointers to help you unravel the night sky. It is useful if you have a compass, but if not, we explain how to find north on page 206.

The brightest object in the night sky is not a star, but a planet: **Venus**. To find it, look west around twilight (when it's known as the Evening Star) or east just before dawn (when it becomes the Morning Star). In between times, another simple planet to identify is **Mars**, which glimmers with a reddish hue.

The brightest star seen from Earth at night is **Sirius** – it's almost twice as brilliant as the next contender (Canopus), so is easily spotted quite low to the south. Sirius is relatively close to us: about 80 trillion miles away. To get an idea of the distance, try to recall what you were doing eight and a half years ago – that's when the light you see from it left the star to travel towards us at 300,000km per second.

On clear nights you may also be able to see the **Milky Way**. Earth is part of the Milky Way – we're situated in one of its spiral arms – but a particularly dense cluster of the galaxy's stars forms a faint band of light like a cloud sweeping across the sky.

Unless you make a wintry trip to the far north of Scotland, you won't see the colourful celestial phenomenon that is the **northern lights** (aurora borealis). However, wherever you are in Britain you should be able to witness a **meteor shower**. These 'shooting stars' are specks of dust burning up as they enter our

chilling

planet's upper atmosphere. Conveniently, meteor showers are annual events so it's easy to know when to look out for them. The summer dates for your diary are 5 May (Eta Aquarids), 28–29 July (Delta Aquarids) and 12–13 August (Perseids – the most spectacular of all). In a leap year, these showers will all be a day earlier.

If you really want to impress your friends, however, you will have to be able to point out the constellations ...

When you're a bit tipsy in a field, the Milky Way looks like this.

1. Cassiopeia

Look north-east and you'll find an unmistakable W formed by five bright stars close together. Cassiopeia takes its name from a mythical queen of Ethiopia whose incorrigible boasting nearly led to her daughter Andromeda being sacrificed to a sea monster.

2. Cygnus (the Swan)

Its other name, the Northern Cross, is more helpful in tracking Cygnus down. Look for a large cross in the north, four stars long (the swan's body) and six across (its wings).

3. Hercules

The fifth largest constellation, Hercules's pelvis is a huge four-star cup shape (actually called the Keystone) in the centre of the sky. His legs (propelling him westward) protrude from the lower two stars, while what looks like two flailing arms emanate from the top two.

4. Orion (the Hunter)

Most quickly identified by finding Orion's belt – a row of three bright stars very close together. Above them to the left, the very bright star is the well-known Betelgeuse (roughly where Orion's head is), while to the right, an arc of stars represents the hunter's shield.

5. Pegasus (the Winged Horse)

Look east for the Great Square of Pegasus – a large four-point diamond trailing strings of stars that, with some imagination, appear vaguely wing-like.

6. Scorpius (the Scorpion)

A large concentration of bright stars in the south marks the scorpion's head. Its body trails magnificently across the sky like a backwards question mark towards its two-pronged sting.

7. Ursa Major (the Great Bear)

Also known as the Plough or the Big Dipper. The seven main stars of Ursa Major form a shape that looks like a saucepan with a long handle.

Fooling a

Baring all

It was Michelangelo who asked the eternal question:
'What spirit is so empty and blind that it cannot recognize the fact that the foot is more noble than the shoe, and skin more beautiful that the garment with which it is clothed?' Or, to put it another way, as did the girl who took it all off (bar a red bandana) at the Isle of Wight festival in 1969, only to be hauled away by security: 'Why can't they let me be what I am? I just wanted to be free.'

Sure enough, there's something about the English summer that makes us want to strip off, whether it's on a deserted Norfolk coast or in front of 100,000 yowling spectators in a Glasto mudlake. There are naturist beaches all around the UK, official or not: from Crakaig in the Highlands right down to Zennor at the tip of Cornwall. There's even a gay one in Snowdonia – 'probably best avoided by families', hints the British Naturism guide.

Most of these are, understandably, quite isolated spots, but people looking to socialise in the buff have lots of options. NudeFest (www.nudefest.co.uk) takes place at a holiday park in Cornwall. It doesn't appear to feature any bands, but attractions include a heated swimming pool, toddlers' play area and aviary, plus the gratifying sight of fields full of sunburnt nude dads bending over to bang in a tent peg. Over in the southeast, the Naturist Foundation (www.naturistfoundation. org) hold a jazz festival in June (no trombone jokes please). Merryhill Leisure Park, 'the UK's premier naturist club', holds its own festival (www.merryhill-leisure.co.uk), this year featuring a Queen tribute act; rather bafflingly, they invite you to turn up in fancy dress (Freddie or Brian), which is surely missing the point. For more hardcore punters, the Sunnybroom Club, a croft and campsite near Aberdeen, is holding a Punk Night in August (www.british-naturism.org/events). Naked Scottish pogoing – the mind boggles.

Even the crowded old cities gets in on the act with the World Naked Bike Ride, which does exactly what it says on the tin. Organised partly to 'celebrate the human body' and partly as a protest against oil dependency, the ride takes place in cities across the world at around the same time each year. Clothing is optional

ound

and creativity is encouraged; it's really quite a sight. Rides are planned in early June in Brighton, Cardiff, London, Manchester, Sheffield, Southampton, York and Edinburgh – although, in Edinburgh's case, the police are threatening to cover up anyone who goes completely starkers. (Hope they don't find out about Sunnybroom's Punk Night, because that could get nasty.) Then there's MotorcycleNudes, who hold summer rallies for naked bikers – yes, they say, even Harley riders. Another one for the calendar is World Naked Gardening Day this month (see page 21). If that's not enough, Abbey House Gardens in Malmesbury, Wiltshire, hosts several 'clothes optional' visitors' days through the summer, and is known for its lovely gardens.

Let it not be said, however, that getting naked can't be cool (in every sense). London boasts a monthly naturist nightclub, Starkers, in Vauxhall. Staff are not in uniform – or anything else – and the organisers promise DJs, yoga demonstrations and, more importantly, well-heated dancefloors.

But for the common or garden streaker, who only unzips when well lubricated with that uniquely British mix of strong cider, fitful sunshine and 20-odd years' worth of emotional repression, there are only two serious options: Wimbledon, or a festival. Leeds seems to top the bill when it comes to nudity – maybe Yorkshire folk really are more hardy – but Glastonbury's Stone Circle is perhaps a more sympathetic place to commune with nature. The Secret Garden Party winks at skinny-dipping in the pond (except if you are too mashed to keep afloat), but Bestival fences off its attractive water feature. Best of all are the festivals near the sea: Beach Break Live (north Cornwall), T4 On the Beach (Weston-super-Mare), and even the highly acclaimed Aldeburgh festival of classical music, where top music critics have been known to rip off their tailcoats and ballgowns to plunge into the North Sea.

Top tips

- Sunscreen is key. You know that old line about sticking it where the sun don't shine? We suggest sticking it there.

- Start with swimming. If you can't quite face whipping off your costume poolside, do it under the water. Mmmm … feels good.

- For the bike: get a comfortable saddle. And clean it first.

- Embarrassed? Don't be. The British love a streaker. Check on YouTube.

- Mud can be bad for you. One American study found that students who often went mud-wrestling were more likely to get dermatitis. And besides, you just don't know what else might be under there.

- Don't offend onlookers. Drunk festivalgoers and very small children may find your naked arse hilarious. Not so security guards. Or, worse, parents.

- Keep an eye on your clothes. You've left your shorts or bra by the side of the main stage, ready to grab if and when you lose your nerve. Think it'll still be there in 10 minutes? Think again.

Carrie O'Grady

Festival People

Tom Pearson
**founder of the
Farmageddon festival**

I'm a GP in London, but my parents are arable farmers in East Anglia. In 2003, I decided to have a party there. It's a really nice setting – a field surrounded by a moat. I had loads of friends in bands, so it was a double-edged decision because I knew that quite often they struggled to get gigs. We created a little website but the first year was effectively a private party with 200-250 people. Everyone said it was a really good laugh, so we did it again the next year.

The reason that Farmageddon works quite well is that it still feels like a private party. I invite quite a small number of people every year, and they email me to see if they can bring a mate, and then their mates email me to see if they can bring a mate. We try really hard to keep it under 400.

It is partly from a licensing point of view, but it's also really nice to keep the numbers down. I knew one girl who organised what she thought was going to be a mini-festival with friends in a band who unexpectedly became a bit famous – she was expecting 300 people and 10,000 turned up. The police had to come along and help, and she ended up facing £20,000 worth of fines. So I'm always a bit wary of that.

The first year it cost £6,000 to put on and I think I ended up £7 down. But I found a bottle of Jack Daniel's in a ditch, so I think that made me even. That was complete guesswork and very lucky. It has got more expensive the years afterwards – last time it cost £14,000 – and we reckon we've had an average £400 loss. Luckily, I share that with my brother who helps me organise it, and we reckon that £200 for a good party is fair enough. We don't

exactly charge for the tickets but there are a bunch of friends dressed up as cowgirls and cowboys who demand what I call non-negotiable donations which started at £25 and are now at about £40.

One of our biggest costs is the loos – you're talking at least £1,200. Apart from that, the marquee costs about £1,000, we pay the lighting and sound guys about £2,600, and I pay the travelling expenses of the bands. I always feel guilty that I can't pay them properly, but we're really not talking about that sort of money.

When will I stop? Well, it's a year-to-year thing. Because we don't pre-sell tickets I can never be sure how many people will turn up, and although we've almost always had great weather, I do worry that one year it will pour down. If a hundred people didn't come, it would suddenly mean a £4,000 loss and that would be quite hard to take. Plus, we're running out of tags. We have a new one every year, and we've already had Acropalypse Now, Livestock, Barn to be Wild, and Dark Side of the Moo.

But lots of the people who come say that it's the highlight of their year, and there's a lot of pressure to keep it going. It keeps us all in touch at a time when we could be drifting apart.

Plus, there are moments of it that I love: Friday night when everyone starts pitching up, Saturday morning when we start decorating everything and making it look beautiful, and about 1am Sunday when I've finally paid all the bands, then my job's sort of done and everything's starting to quieten down. Of course, that never lasts for long.

Dish of the

Steak, ale and horseradish pie

From Big Chill regulars Pure Pie

pure pie

Serves 6

For the filling:
1kg chuck steak
1 large onion
200g field
   mushrooms
2 medium potatoes
3 tsp vegetable oil
400ml water
1 veal stock cube
2 tsp tomato puree
1 heaped tbsp
   beef demi-glace
   (available online,
   or use a good
   beef stock that
   you have reduced
   down)

200ml Murphy's
   Irish stout
2 tsp creamed
   horseradish
2 tbsp chopped
   parsley
Salt to season

For the lid:
300g puff pastry
1 egg yolk
1 tsp milk

Method:

- Start by trimming your steak of all fat before dicing into half-inch cubes and then setting to one side. Peel your onion and roughly dice. Heat a good-sized, heavy-bottomed pan and add your oil. Heat a few more seconds, then add the diced steak. Fry until it has taken on colour, then add the onions.

- In a separate container, mix the water, tomato puree and veal stock before adding to the steak and onion mix. Put a lid on the pan and bring to the boil, then turn down to simmer.

- Peel your potatoes and dice them into quarter-inch cubes. Leave in water until needed, then slice your mushrooms about a quarter-inch thick and set to one side.

- After the steak has simmered for 40 minutes, add the ale and simmer for a further 20 minutes before adding the potatoes and mushrooms. Cook for another 10 minutes and check potatoes, which should now be al dente. If they are still too hard, cook until you reach the desired texture. Add the horseradish and stir in well.

- To finish, mix the beef demi-glace with a little cold water to form a paste and then add to the pie mix slowly, stirring continuously to avoid lumps forming. Stir in parsley, then taste and season with salt as required before transferring to a suitable oval pie dish, ideally holding 1.7-2litres.

- Once this has cooled, roll out puff pastry and top the pie. Brush with 1 egg yolk mixed with milk and cook in a pre-heated oven at gas mark 4/175C/350F for 35 minutes or until hot and golden brown.

Drink of th

Big Chill punch

From the Big Chill bartenders

Pour the ingredients into a glass and **fill it up** with rocks of ice. **Cover** and **shake**, fill up with more ice if needed and **top up** with champagne. **Garnish** with a slice of lemon.

20ml lemon juice
20ml peach and passion
 fruit syrup
20ml white peach puree
25ml vodka
Champagne

e month

Game of

The human snail race

Organised snail races have been a huge hit at the Big Chill festival, and with just a few sleeping bags and a handful of jumpers, it's easy to set up your own.

Preparing the course is the first, and easiest, task. Find a dry, mud-free patch of grass and mark out a start and finish line, about 10 metres apart, using jumpers, spare guy-ropes, lengths of string, or anything else you have to hand. Getting all the contestants to the starting line is the next challenge – each must be completely inside a sleeping bag with just their head sticking out, lying face-forwards on their front. Most will fall over trying to wriggle into this position, and everyone will look silly.

With a bit of imagination the creative members of the group can transform the sleeping bags into snail costumes – pillows tied on to contestants' backs make excellent shells, and a strip of card and two twigs or pipe cleaners can be easily turned into a pair of antennae with a bit of sticky tape. You could make the race more interesting by insisting that the winning snail must cross the finish line with both shell and antennae intact, but, as you will discover, that is much harder said than done.

Some people get the hang of human snail racing straight away and make a swift dash to the finish line (the elbow-and-knees crawl is a particularly successful technique), while others just can't seem to do any more than squirm about helplessly at the start line. Whether you take part, or just sit back and watch, it is a hilarious way to pass an hour or two.

Perri Lewis

May festival directory

MUSIC

THE BIG ONES

All Tomorrow's Parties
When: Mid May
Where: Butlin's Holiday Camp, Minehead, Somerset
Cost: festival ticket including accommodation £318 for twin room.
Website: www.atpfestival.com
This two-weekend festival kicks off the season in style with chalet accommodation (lucky, because there's lots of sand). And if you get tired of listening to the stellar line-up there are Butlin's Splash Waterworld and fast-food outlets galore.

The Great Escape
When: Mid May
Where: Brighton
Cost: £45 for a saver ticket, £150 for delegate ticket inc etnry to TGE convention.
Website: www.escapegreat.com
Three day event at venues across Brighton and Hove with vast number of performers playing in clubs, pubs and even people's front rooms. Venues may be small but the bands aren't: the result is a festival that is both civilised and intimate.

ROCK/INDIE

The Celtic Rally Fest
When: Early May
Where: Maker Heights, Cornwall
Cost: £80 gold ticket, £60 silver ticket, £30 day ticket

Website: www.beerfestivalevents.co.uk
One for the boys, this. Four days of beers, bikes, cars, historical re-enactments and live bands. Discover your Blitz spirit by quaffing ales in bars themed to recreate war-torn London.

Frodsham Festival
When: Mid/Late May
Where: Frodsham, Cheshire
Cost: around £30
Website: www.frodshamfestival.co.uk
Tired of soulless mega festivals? Go to the other extreme with this newbie organised by a former Glastonbury roadie. You're unlikely to lose your mates. It all takes place in the town's craft centre.

Glastonbudget
When: Mid/May
Where: Wymeswold, Leicestershire
Cost: Adult around £40; aged 16-17 £37.50; child £25.50; and under 5s are £1.
Website: www.glastonbudget.co.uk
Like Glastonbury in a parallel universe where the bands seem strangely familiar – Razorlike, Antarctic Monkeys, Four Fighters etc – but everything is cheap as chips. Tribute bands and new music, often with authentically Glastonbury-ish mud.

Lowender Festival
When: Early May
Where: Colliford Lake Park, Cornwall
Cost: adult weekend ticket £40, children £10
Website: www.lowender.co.uk
Is it the cider or is that a gigantically oversized slide over there? It's either complete madness or total genius but this festival dedicated to local talent takes place in a

park with go-carting, boating lakes and death slides. Wheee.

Nice & Sleazy
When: Mid May
Where: Morecombe, Lancashire
Cost: weekend ticket £25 with free camping
Website: www.bigivanpromotions.moonfruit.com
Like a flock of exotic birds, a thousand punks go to Morecombe to compare make up and mosh about to alternative, ska and new wave bands. Small, friendly and now with an outdoor acoustic stage.

Wychwood Music Festival
When: End May
Where: Cheltenham Racecourse, Gloucestershire
Cost: Adults around £100 with camping; youth/concession £72; campervans £30
Website: www.wychwoodfestival.com
A bijou event offering an impressive mix of big names – Supergrass, Martha Wainwright, Mr Scruff etc – and a renowned family friendly vibe. The festival connoisseur's way to start the season.

DANCE/ELECTRONICA

The Great Escape
When: Mid/May
Where: venues in Brighton, East Sussex
Cost: Adults £35-£50
Website: www.escapegreat.com
Seaside showcase of the hippest new bands – think The Ting, Tings and The Big Pink – now you can see next year's big thing before the rest of us. Skinny jeans and an insouciant look obligatory.

Liverpool Sound City
When: Mid/Late May
Where: Hard Days Night Hotel and multiple venues in Liverpool
Cost: around £5-£10 for a concert to £65 for all evening shows and events, £150 for full pass
Website: www.liverpoolsoundcity.co.uk

Promising sweaty days, steamy nights and a conference for music biz folk and fans, this has every genre you can shake a drumstick at – indie, electro, acoustic, hip hop, rock, emo…

Run to the Sun
When: Mid/Late May
Where: Porth, Newquay, Cornwall
Cost: Adult around £75, children: £37.50
Website: www.runtothesun.co.uk
An anything goes mixture of VW campervans, beach culture, DJs and light shows in the UK's surfing capital. Catch the likes of Lisa Lashes and Goldie and parade your beloved VW at the Show 'n' Shine.

FOLK

Acoustic Festival of Britain
When: Mid/Late May
Where: Catton Hall, Walton-on-Trent, South Derbyshire
Cost: Adult weekend around £90; with camping around £100
Website: www.acousticfestival.co.uk
If you no longer consider bleeding eardrums to be a sign that you're having a good time, this one's for you. Festival favourites like Jethro Tull, Donovan, Deacon Blue and the Animals, but all nicely unplugged.

Bearded Theory
When: Mid May
Where: Near Ashbourne, Derbyshire
Cost: £45 for a weekend ticket
Website: www.beardedtheory.co.uk
Five stages, a medieval market village and a beard styling parlour for the unrepentantly furry-of-face, which is such a magnificently good idea it must surely catch on around the folk circuit.

Chester Folk Festival
When: Late May
Where: Kelsall, nr. Chester, Cheshire
Cost: around £50; 10–18 years, half price
Website: www.chesterfolk.org.uk/
Mostly based in the field behind the Morris Dancer pub and at other watering holes in

Like your festivals with a touch of 'grand'? Liverpool Sound City it is!

the village it's a safe bet you'll sink a few pints before the weekend is over. Organised by local folk enthusiasts.

Chippenham Folk Festival

When: Mid/Late May
Where: Chippenham, Wiltshire
Cost: around £70
Website: www.chippfolk.co.uk
Every May for the past forty years this historic town has turned itself into a great big party. No pub, tearoom or hall is left untouched by the music, storytelling, dancing and infectious conviviality.

Clennell Hall Folk Festival

When: Mid May
Where: Alwinton, Northumberland
Cost: Adult around £30
Website: www.clennellhallhotel.com/id19.html
Endearingly grassroots – organisers try to make sure performers don't end up out of pocket for appearing – expect folksiness with a Northumbrian flavour and a lot of foot stomping.

Cottingham Springboard Music Festival

When: Late May
Where: Hull, East Yorkshire
Cost: FREE
Website: www.springboard.bravehost.com
Costing you zilch in ticket prices – and with over one hundred acts appearing that's something of a bargain – the venues are all pubs so you can safely assume the weekend is unlikely to cost you nothing at all.

Dart Music Festival

When: Early May
Where: Dartmouth, South Devon
Cost: Mostly FREE although contributions welcomed
Website: www.dartmusicfestival.co.uk
A genre-busting weekend with everything from boogie-woogie and jazz to school orchestras and opera singing. It's all free but expect to have a bucket shaken in your direction at some point.

Dunstaffnage Music Festival

When: Late May
Where: Oban, Scotland
Cost: around £60 weekend ticket including camping
Website: www.dunstaffnagemusicfestival.co.uk
Never mind the music, check out that sunset. What was once just Pikey's Party (it was his birthday and he fancied a big get together) is now a proper festival loved for its dramatic skies and island views.

The Gathering

When: Early May
Where: Instow, North Devon
Cost: £25 weekend (includes camping), 10–15 years £10
Website: www.efestivals.co.uk/festivals/didjefest/thegathering
Now who wouldn't enjoy a two-day didgeridoo open mic and jam session? No, really, performers and amateurs alike join together for the love of the didge and mix it up together. Egalitarian fun.

Holmfirth Festival

When: Early May
Where: Holmfirth, West Yorkshire
Cost: Most concerts free. Sat night and Ceilidh £6–£15
Website: www.holmfirthfestivaloffolk.co.uk
This one is all about music and community, so while most events are free you're still getting superior musicianship from the likes of the Eliza Carthy Band and the Peatbog Faeries.

Ireby Music Festival

When: Mid/Late May
Where: Ireby, Cumbria
Cost: £30 for the weekend, 10-16 yr olds £12. Day tickets available
Website: www.musicinireby.co.uk
By all means stop for cake at the WI hall but don't expect everything to be so genteel. With headliners like the Eddie Reader Band, electronic skiffle and explosive fiddle playing, the music is sure to be joyously loud.

Knockengorroch World Ceilidh
When: Thursday Mid/Late May
Where: Carsphairn, Kirkubrightshire, Scotland
Cost: around £80 for 4 days
Website: www.knockengorroch.org.uk
Timed to take place before the midges get going for the summer (be very thankful), there's willow wattling alongside the world music. Unpretentious outdoorsy fun, this is Celtic style partying for the down to earth.

Off The Tracks Spring Festival
When: Mid/Late May
Where: Castle Donington, Leicestershire
Cost: £55 for w/e including camping; children (12-16) £27.50
Website: www.offthetracks.co.uk
An intimate vibe, atmospheric surroundings and a mixture of roots, global, trance and dance. There's also an energy orchard, which sounds just the ticket if the forty-five real ales on offer have left you a little jaded.

Ryedale Folk Weekend
When: Mid/Late May
Where: Ryedale Folk Museum, Hutton le Hole, North Yorskhire
Cost: £40 for a weekend ticket
Website: www.festivalonthemoor.co.uk/ ryedalelweekend/index.htm
With a stream just big enough for paddling, an ice cream parlour and a couple of pubs, this is Five Go Folk Festivalling in Yorkshire. Absurdly picturesque old fashioned fun.

Shepley Spring Festival
When: Mid May
Where: Shepley Village, nr Huddersfield, West Yorkshire
Cost: Adult around £45; youth weekend (11-16) £29; children (11 and under) Free
Website: www.shepleyspringfestival.com
Where else but at a village folk festival would you find a fire-eating pensioner and traditional clog dance troupes with names like Inclognito? Plenty of decent bands too, we should add.

CLASSICAL/JAZZ

Lufthansa Festival of Baroque Music
When: Mid/Late May
Where: Harpenden, Herts
Cost: See website
Website: www.lufthansafestival.org.uk
Celebrating a specific one hundred year slice of musical history, programmes typically include soloists and ensembles from around the world performing little known works alongside masterpieces.

Swaledale Festival
When: Late May/Early June
Where: Various small venues in the dales, near Richmond, N. Yorkshire
Cost: Events are individually priced
Website: www.swaledale-festival.org.uk
A little bit of everything – classical, choral, jazz, world music, art workshops, guided walks, open mic poetry, steel bands, theatre – and the odd lecture from big hitters like Sir Roy Strong.

INTERNATIONAL

PinkPop
When: Late May/Early June
Where: Landgraaf, Netherlands. (near Heerlen)
Cost: around 130 euros
Website: www.pinkpop.org.uk
Anyone who's anyone has played here over the past 40 years – from Pearl Jam to Robbie Williams, Springsteen to Sugababes. Spare a thought for the oldies. They've been relegated to a spin off called Pinkpop Classic. Harsh.

ARTS

Brighton Festival
When: Early/Mid May
Where: Various venues throughout Brighton and Hove
Cost: Events are variously priced, some outdoor events are free
Website: www.brightonfestival.org

As the largest arts festival in England, expect an international selection of exclusive events in music, literature, theatre and dance. If all that isn't enough, be sure to catch an Artist Open House event. What better opportunity to buy a masterpiece - and have a good snoop around artist's living rooms, too!

Burns an' a that!
When: Mid/Late May
Where: Ayr and Ayrshire
Cost: Prices range from free to £20
Website: burns.visitscotland.com/festival
As well as a chance to recite funny sounding poetry and agree how relevant it still is today, you can also enter Scotland's largest coarse fishing competition or try out at the battle of the bands.

Bury St Edmunds Festival
When: Early/Mid May
Where: Theatre Royal plus some outdoor events around the town
Cost: Events individually priced
Website: www2.buryfreepress.co.uk/festival/index.asp

The theme here seems to be, well... just loads of stimulating events in the one place – classical proms, drive in movies, gardening workshops, opera, comedy, world champion kite flying, stand up comedy...

Dulwich Festival
When: Early/Mid May
Where: Dulwich, London
Cost: Many events free
Website: www.dulwichfestival.co.uk
Anyone who thinks London has no sense of community should head to Dulwich in May where an army of volunteers pull together a great little festival of arts, crafts, food, drink, music and street performance.

Dumfries and Galloway Arts Festival
When: Late May
Where: Various locations throughout the region
Cost: Events individually priced, some are free

Arts of all kinds are celebrated – and for sale – at Brighton Festival.

Relax with a good book or two at the Guardian Hay Festival.

Website: www.dgartsfestival.org.uk
An annual influx of international arty types and culture vultures spice up life in one of Scotland's most rural regions. World premiers, touring theatre, music etc in venues scattered across the countryside.

Futuresonic Live
When: Mid May
Where: Manchester
Cost: expect around £45 for a weekend ticket
Website: www.futuresonic.com
Out there in the Tomorrow's World of art, music and ideas you'll find genres you've never heard of (math rock, Italo disco anyone?), debates that will bake your noodle and chin-stroking art happenings.

Hampstead and Highgate Festival
When: Early May
Where: London
Cost: See website
Website: www.hamandhighfest.co.uk
Don't even think about pitching your tent on Hampstead Heath. This is a refined affair with a reputation for musical excellence and big literary names, hosted in two of London's most picturesque villages.

Salisbury International Arts Festival
When: Late May/Early June
Where: Salisbury, Wiltshire
Cost: Varies from FREE to around £20
Website: www.salisburyfestival.co.uk
Expect lots of juicy offerings and famous faces – Julian Lloyd Webber, Vikram Seth, Jon Snow, er, Bonnie Langford – plus a rare chance to watch performances sitting inside Stonehenge itself.

LITERATURE/WRITTEN WORD

The Chalfont St Giles and Jordans Literary Festival
When: Mid May
Where: Chalfont St Giles
Cost: See website

Website: www.chalfontstgilesliteraryfestival. org.uk

Where there are authors dispensing tricks of the trade there are audiences of hopefuls waiting to discover the secret of how to make it off the slush pile. This one tantalises further with a writing competition.

Daphne Du Maurier Festival
When: Early/Mid May
Where: Fowey Hall, St Austell town, Cornwall
Cost: Events at various prices
Website: www.dumaurierfestival.co.uk
Don't sit there dreaming about going to Manderley, get yourself to the Cornish Riviera and explore the real locations behind some of the UK's favourite novels, plus talks from other much loved writers, comedians and broadcasters.

The Guardian Hay Festival
When: Late May
Where: Hay-on-Wye, Herefordshire
Cost: Many events are free, most ticketed gigs range from £5-£19
Website: www.hayfestival.com
Singleton bookworms take heart. Hay offers literary giants, international celebrities and the chance of wedding bells. Apparently twenty-eight couples whose eyes met over a paperback have since got hitched. Not a bad record.

Hexham Book Festival
When: Early May
Where: Queen's Hall, Hexham, Northumberland
Cost: See website
Website: www.hexhambookfestival.co.uk
A newish name on the ever-growing circuit offering the likes of Janet Street-Porter, Will Self and Sophie Grigson plus noteworthy extras including hospital and rural reading groups and screenwriting workshops.

Lincoln Book Festival
When: Early/mid May
Where: Most events at Lincoln Drill Hall
Cost: See website

Website: www.lincolnbookfestival.co.uk
Wine tasting, writing workshops, stand up comedy and authors in conversation – Iain Banks, John Hedley, Paddy Ashdown etc – what's a booklover to do but just write off May and add Lincoln to their to-do list.

Linton Children's Book Festival
When: Early May
Where: Library, Linton, Cambridgeshire
Cost: Free, but booking necessary
Website: www.lintonbookfest.org
Have a break and pack the kids off to puppet shows, talks by favourite authors, Poohsticks trails and such like. Everything's free so they could be kept busy for a whole week. They'll be happy, you'll be happy…

Poetry Next to the Sea
When: Early May
Where: Wells next-to-the-Sea, Norfolk
Cost: See website
Website: www.poetry-next-the-sea.com
Unpublished Norfolk poets, set your words free and bag some cash. For those who don't win the annual competition, maybe pick up some tips from workshops with the pros and try again next year?

Swindon Festival of Literature
When: Runs throughout May
Where: Swindon Central Library and other locations around the town
Cost: Events at various prices
Website: www.swindonfestivalofliterature. co.uk
Pass the smelling salts, these are the kind of names that set festivalling hearts aflutter – Sir David Attenborough, Margaret Drabble, John Pilger – all kicked off with Morris dancing and a hot brekkie. Perfect.

Wordfringe
When: Runs throughout May
Where: Various locations in Aberdeen and Aberdeenshire
Cost: See website
Website: www.wordfringe.co.uk
Devoted to new writing, local reading circles and bookworms descend on venues across

the region to hear extracts from brand new work and pick up tips on how to improve their own scribblings.

Word – University of Aberdeen Writer's Fest

When: Mid May
Where: Aberdeen
Cost: Events priced individually
Website: www.abdn.ac.uk/word/

Head north, word lovers, to the granite city where you can while away the days and nights with authors, poets, broadcasters, filmmakers, storytellers, book obsessives and hoards of bookish kids.

Young Readers Birmingham

When: Mid May
Where: Birmingham
Cost: See website
Website: www.birmingham.gov.uk/youngreaders.bcc

For kids whose noses are permanently stuck in a book here's a chance to meet favourite writers and characters, be read endless stories and spend happy hours browsing bookstalls. Keeps them quiet anyway.

OUTDOORS

Isle of Wight Walking Festival

When: Mid May
Where: All over the Isle of Wight
Cost: Walks are either free or priced at £12
Website: www.isleofwightwalkingfestival.co.uk

Walking, but not the pedestrian kind. Try marching over hot coals or speed dating as you hike (three weddings in the bag so far). Even the more conventional walks have stunning island views and lots of good banter.

ALTERNATIVE ENTERTAINMENT

Beltane Fire Festival

When: Evening of 30th April/1st May
Where: Calton Hill, Edinburgh
Cost: Free entry to procession
Website: www.beltane.org

Strip naked, paint yourself red and dance in a frenzy round a massive bonfire. No? Okay, watch the Lords and Ladies of Misrule doing it instead in this annual burn-up to celebrate the start of summer.

Cheese Rolling

When: Late May Bank Holiday Monday
Where: Cooper's Hill, 4 km south of Gloucester
Cost: Free entrance and entry to the competitions
Website: www.cheese-rolling.co.uk

A quaint country tradition that requires mountain rescue, St John's Ambulance and a line of rugby players to catch hurtling competitors. Do you really want to hurl yourself down a vertical hill to win a cheese? Hundreds do every year.

Downton Cuckoo Fair

When: First May bank holiday weekend
Where: Downton, Wiltshire (nr Salisbury)
Cost: Free entry to town centre
Website: www.cuckoofair.co.uk

With the arrival of the first cuckoo in the village comes good weather (supposedly) and 20,000 people looking for maypole dancing, bingo, cream teas, clay pigeon shooting and other villagey fete type activities.

Helston Furry Dance

When: May 8th (unless date falls on Sunday or Monday, when it is held the preceding Saturday)
Where: Helston, Cornwall
Cost: Free

Website: www.helston-online.co.uk
Not a troupe of hairy dancers or people dressed as animals but actually a rather pretty spring festival – a flora dance – which sees the town decked with bluebells and flags, and dancing from dawn til dusk.

Obby Oss Festival

When: 1st May (or 2nd if 1st is a Sunday)
Where: Padstow, Cornwall – throughout the town
Cost: Free
Website: www.padstow.com/obby_oss/obby_oss.php
A ritual that sees the locals dress in white and two 'obby 'osses (that's hobby horses to the rest of us) processing through the streets trying to nab young maidens. Celebrations go on until the 'osses turn in at 10 o'clock.

Tetbury Wool Sack Race

When: Late May Bank Holiday Monday
Where: Tetbury town centre
Cost: Individual entry is £5, team entry is £20. Spectating is free
Website: www.tetburywoolsack.co.uk
Once an opportunity for 17th century lads to impress the ladies – whose head isn't turned by the sight of a man puffing up a hill with a sack on his back? – nowadays it's a charity race plus fair, market and street performances.

FOOD & DRINK

The British Asparagus Festival

When: Runs throughout May into early June
Where: Evesham and Breforton town centres and public houses, Worcestershire
Cost: Events individually priced. Roaming around associated farmers markets is free
Website: www.britishasparagusfestival.org
Oh the joys of a festival devoted to a single food. Grown men dressed as asparagus tips, people having their future told by the UK's only Asparamancer, asparagus being delivered to the Houses of Parliament by vintage car, that kind of thing.

English Wine Week

When: Late May
Where: Vineyards and winerys throughout Britain
Cost: Events individually priced
Website: www.englishwineweek.co.uk; www.devonwineweek.co.uk
For those who still scoff at the idea of quality English wine (you curs), here's a whole week to change your minds. Take a boozy stagger through some the UK's finest vineyards.

Henley Food Festival

When: Mid May
Where: Town centre, Henley-on-Thames
Cost: £6.50 per adult day ticket, under 16s are free
Website: www.henleyfoodfestival.co.uk
Think of this less as an excuse to stuff your face for two days, more as a chance to hone your culinary skills and discover exciting new ingredients. Who are we kidding? Just don't eat for a week before then get stuck in.

Watercress Festival

When: Early/Mid May
Where: Town centre, Alresford, Hampshire
Cost: Free entry to most events
Website: www.watercress.co.uk/festival
A whole week of watercress love with celebrity chefs, Morris dancing and a chance to beat the local record of eating six bags of the stuff in two minutes, after which you may wish to sit down and not look at any watercress for a while.

Emma McGowan

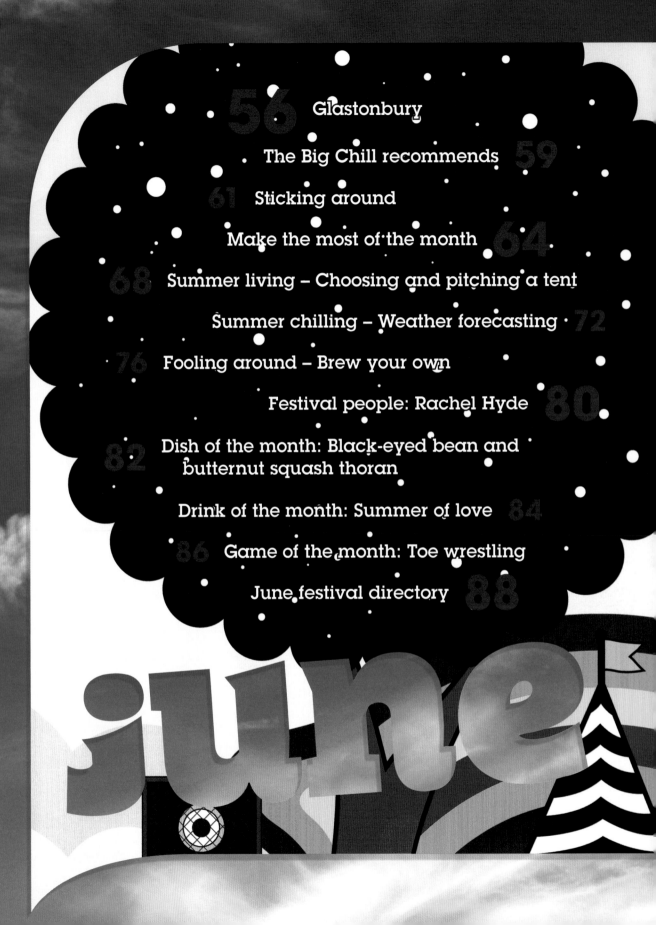

june

'Diverse delirium' – Stu Scannell

illustration Brett Wilkinson

Glasto

Somerset

www.glastonburyfestivals.co.uk

Other festivals might boast plusher facilities or hipper crowds, but the one thing that Glastonbury unequivocally does better than any other event is mythology. Reading is the festival where artists famously get bottled off (one suspects Meat Loaf rues his decision to demand of a restive crowd, 'Do you wanna rock'n'roll or do you wanna throw shit?' to this day). Glastonbury is the festival where an angel, or at the very least, a 'bioluminescent life form' is reputed to have appeared by the side of the stage in 1971 and been addressed by the MC. 'Whatever you are – talk to us,' he pleaded, but it vanished, perhaps after noting the state of the toilet facilities.

People talk in hushed tones of Benicassim, the Spanish seaside festival where the sun always shines, the lineup is impossibly stellar and you get carried around in a sedan chair while dining off handmade ravioli of foie gras and black truffle. But the one thing Benicassim doesn't seem to have is an equivalent of the famous Glastonbury Moment when the music and the setting combine to spine-tingling effect, and the artist providing the soundtrack almost invariably experiences a subsequent surge in sales and standing: in 2008, a Glastonbury Moment broadcast live on television helped fast-track Elbow from alt-rock also-rans to national-treasure status.

The mythology and indeed the Moment come about as a result of Glastonbury's unique atmosphere that in turn derives from a confluence of location, history, hedonism and sheer scale. Even if you don't buy the stories about ley lines and the Holy Grail being buried nearby, Glastonbury's site is bucolic and beautiful and cut

NO TIME TO WASTE

onbury

Glasto's unique atmosphere derives from a confluence of location, history, hedonism and sheer scale.

The bongo. A firm Glastonbury festival-goer favourite. Except maybe at 3am...

off from the world in a way that is magical when the sun shines, and a living hell when it's lashing down and you've had enough and you're trying to get off it to find a taxi to take you back to civilisation. The festival has its roots in the Age of Aquarius – it began in 1970 and soon developed into an intermittent free event known as Glastonbury Fayre. Although it didn't become the kind of cultural talking point it is today until the 80s, something of the earlier era still doggedly clings to the event. In its most prosaic, this manifests itself in clouds of dope smoke, terrible clothes and the naked hippy sitting amid festival refuse that you will inevitably see at some point during the festival, but there's also a certain musical open-mindedness in the crowd: you get the feeling that poor old Meat Loaf would have had a better time had he been booked to play the Pyramid Stage.

Glastonbury can be intimidating to the neophyte: it seems to go on for ever with fields and fields packed not just with music but comedy, theatre, political debate, craft workshops and stone circles. You could try to plan your weekend to take in all the big names on the main stages if you want, but be warned, you

THE BIGCHILL
recommends

RockNess

Dores, near Inverness,
Scotland www.rockness.co.uk

The name RockNess summons up the image of a writhing beast emerging from a doomy, fathomless lake and yet this Scottish festival – still in its infancy, but a runaway success – has an amazingly danceable lineup, attracting everyone from bouncy electro superstars to jangling indie poseurs. Daft Punk's headlining gig in 2007 proved so popular that they had to take the sides off the tent so that more people could see.

With headliners such as the Prodigy and Basement Jaxx you could start to think that this is just another run of the mill big hitter, but make no mistake: this is one festival that's proud of its heritage. In the smaller tents, Scottish indie bands such as the Dykeenies and the 1990s compete for A&R eyeballs. The stars get into the spirit, too. When Norman Cook played a three-hour set, he strode on stage bearing a saltire. Local boy Mylo delighted the crowds by mixing traditional Scottish music into his DJ set. And to top it all off, why not end your night with a trip to the haggis van to get your festival fill.

Even the DJ tent is patriotic, as befits a festival that's so well tailored to people who love to get wrecked and dance. (Rob da Bank, who curates Bestival, expressed amazement at how enthusiastic the RockNess punters can be: 'I started playing at 4.30 in the afternoon,' he recalled. 'In England, no one would be dancing until, you know, 8. But up here, everyone's totally up for it.')

Of course, there's much more to enjoy here than just beats and breaks. In an idyllic setting on the shores of the famous loch, RockNess has scenery to delight even the most jaded eyes. And there'll be plenty of time to appreciate it, too - at this time of year, the sun rises at 4.15am and doesn't set until after 10pm. Don't forget the sun cream.

Mind you, it's not all good news. First, there are the country's famous midges, then the drinks at 'London prices' (£3.20 for a pint), a serious dearth of healthy eateries and, perhaps worst of all, over-refreshed locals repeatedly shouting the chorus of the Automatic's only hit: 'What's that coming over the hill – is it a monster?' At the rate it's growing, RockNess is turning into a monster indeed.
Carrie O'Grady

won't be able to stick to it: one of your party will get lost, which isn't quite the trauma that it once was in the days before mobile phones, but you will still spend ages waiting for them, which will throw off your carefully laid plans completely. In any case, there's an argument that says that the big names on the main stages aren't really what Glastonbury is about, and if you want to experience the breadth of the festival, the best thing to do is abandon all thought of a schedule, pick a couple of must-see acts and spend the rest of the time just wandering around, seeing what you find. After all, Glastonbury-goers can be many things – elated, overwhelmed, miserable, under the influence of so many mind-bending substances that they're convinced they are Phil Collins or Frederick I of Prussia – but the one thing they very seldom are, is bored.

Alexis Petridis

You might as well embrace it ... Glastonbury mud games are GO!

Sticking around

Glastonbury and North Somerset

So Glastonbury-lovers, after sharing your personal space with more than 150,000 other carousing festival-goers for five days at one of the biggest music events in the world, what you need now, besides a shower and a good lie down, is some quiet time in the rolling Somerset countryside.

WHERE TO CAMP

Not far from Glastonbury in the pretty village of Burtle, Orchard Camping offers pitches in the apple tree garden next to Ye Olde Burtle Inn. With views of the Somerset Levels, Glastonbury Tor, Polden Hill and the Mendips, this is a hidden gem. Facilities include free hot showers, a small shop, children's play area, an indoor games room and a pub. Surrounded by nature reserves and open countryside to explore in all directions, Orchard Camping is the perfect festival antidote.
www.burtleinn.fsnet.co.uk/Camping4.htm

WHAT TO DO

Walking

From the top of the 518ft Glastonbury Tor, you'll be able to see most of the Levels. Through town, country, Tor and ravine, whether you find the Holy Grail or not, you'll have had a good walk (5.5km).
www.westcountrywalks.com/exmoor-wsomerset/somersetlevels/glastonbury/Glastonbury.pdf

Swimming

The River Isle at Ilford Bridge in Ilminster comprises shallow and deeper pools, perfect for either paddling or getting in a few strokes. For a fun family day out, head to Warleigh Weir in Claverton where you can take a refreshing dip, a longer swim upstream or sunbathe in the meadow beyond the river.
www.outdoorswimmingsociety.com

Be king of all you survey from Glastonbury Tor.

Wild spot

Near Glastonbury you will come across Ham Wall RSPB nature reserve, which is host to many resident and migratory birds and other wildlife. In the summer you could see bearded tits, water voles, otters, starlings and much more.
www.rspb.org/reserves/guide/h/hamwall/about.asp

The area around Glastonbury was once covered by sea and joined to the mainland by a peninsula, with only the Glastonbury Tor and surrounding land rising above the waves. Today the area is still, in parts, a prolific marshland. Shapwick Heath National Nature Reserve forms part of a great wetland. Its fens and other habitat are host to aquatic plants and creatures, insects, birds and even a star attraction – otters. Also of interest are the remains of an ancient Neolithic track (the oldest found in Britain) and the remains of the peat-extraction industry, which was carried out here until the early 90s.
www.english-nature.org.uk/special/nnr/nnr_details.asp?NNR_ID=141

We dare you

If you're neither acrophobic nor claustrophobic and fancy a challenge, Cheddar Gorge is also the perfect place to try caving or abseiling. Plunge into the depths of the earth under the guidance of a RockSport supervisor, or, make your careful way down 50ft cliff-face. Or both.
www.cheddarcaves.co.uk

If it rains

A cave is the perfect place to take shelter. A cave with cheese inside is even better. The caves in Chedder Gorge comprise 1/2km of cathedral-like chambers carved out by ice-age meltwaters that were once home to our ancestors 40,000 years ago. Fascinating, but cheese monsters will be impatient to get to the shop in town, led by their noses. Copious amounts of cave-matured cheddar are waiting for them to try and buy. Then nibble all the way home. For a child-orientated alternative cave experience, take the kids to Wookey Hole.
www.cheddarcaves.co.uk
www.cheddargorgecheeseco.co.uk

FOOD AND DRINK

Beer

Where better in the UK to find traditional ale than in county that has a town by the name of 'Beer'? The Cotleigh Brewery in Wiveliscombe produces the original Tawny bitter, Barn Owl premium ale, Golden Seahawk and Buzzard dark ale, among others. The brewery and its patrons also proudly put their money where their ale is and have supported the Hawk and Owl Trust for many years, helping to raise funds and awareness about the conservation needs of these majestic birds.
www.cotleighbrewery.com

Not at all cheesy: the road through Cheddar Gorge seen from above.

Wine

Oatley vineyard in Cannington near the Bristol Channel is a 'small but ambitious' winery that was planted in 1986. It's already produced a few award-winning bottles and is managed in an eco-friendly manner. The winery can only organise tours and tastings in small numbers, so call ahead to arrange.
www.oatleyvineyard.co.uk

Local produce

Glastonbury's popular farmers' market is known for an impressive selection of local organic meat, vegetables, cheese, preserves and honey.
www.sfmdirect.co.uk/markets/index.asp?id=5&u=3184336

FOR THE KIDS

The SeaQuarium at Weston Super Mare is situated on the beach surrounded by three miles of sand. It features an underwater shark tunnel and an open-top ray zone where you can see these graceful creatures up close when they come to the surface. Try to get there for feeding time.
www.seaquarium.co.uk/weston.php

The vicious seahorse – finally tamed at Weston's SeaQuarium.

june

Make the most of the month

Dive

Even the most experienced divers might quail at the idea of going into icy Scottish waters, but an opportunity to explore shipwrecks off the Orkney Islands coast could change their minds. Scapa Flow is the graveyard of the German navy. It was confined there after the country's defeat in the first world war and in June 1919, their commander, Rear Admiral Ludwig von Reuter, fearing the fleet would be divided among allied powers, gave the order for the ships to be scuttled. Most went under despite British efforts to save them. There are dozens of other wrecks in the area, some with equally haunting stories.
www.scapascuba.co.uk

Gawp

The East Beach Cafe must be one of the most unusual beach bars in the world. Shaped like a huge copper shell with inspiring views of Littlehampton beach in West Sussex, it is both jaw-dropping to look at and beautifully tranquil to sit inside. The menu is full of locally sourced goodies like wild mushrooms on toast with Sussex gouda, and ranges from fish and chips to pheasant or lamb. A weird and wonderful jewel.
www.eastbeachcafe.co.uk

Scramble

Clambering up and down slopes, falling off bridges, whisking down slides: if you have children and you're in need of a place to utterly wear them out (and yourself besides), Bewilderwood, near Norwich, is the place to go. This huge eco-park rambles through woods and streams, and attractions include zip wires, mazes and tree-top villages. Mud and fun seem to be the main components.
www.bewilderwood.co.uk

Be inspired

It is just possible that you are already attending five evening classes while simultaneously finishing off your doctorate and bringing up two children. If that's not the case, you might consider the odd refresher course for your mind. This is where Schumacher College comes in. In the beautiful setting of Dartington Hall in Dorset, the college specialises in short courses on subjects connected to the environment and matters spiritual. You can travel with Satish Kumar to Dartmoor to contemplate Gaia theory and natural beauty, or learn about the work of economist EF Schumacher who tried to warn us that we were going the wrong way more than three decades ago.
www.schumachercollege.org.uk

Imbibe

As someone very wise once said: 'Wine is constant proof that God loves us and wants to keep us happy. At Grape Inventions in Bath, Ian and Pat, both huge lovers of wine, have worked out an interesting way to increase their visitors' understanding: they run tasting sessions and then help you to make up a version of the wine you liked most. You mix grape juices and the yeasts into the fermenting vessels, go away for a few weeks, then come back with your own designs for the labels for a bottling session.
www.grapeinventions.co.uk/faq.htm

Watch

Rowena Cade must have been one of the most stubborn, single-minded women in the UK. Her dream of building an outdoor theatre on the cliffs of Cornwall was realised only after decades of backbreaking work: she and her gardener Billy Rawlings literally built it stone by stone. The result is one of the most spectacular small theatres in the world: audience members sit with their backs to the cliff while the play unfolds before the backdrop of the ever-changing Atlantic. How do set designers manage? They must yearn to bring on a storm for King Lear and a sunny sky for As You Like It. The magnificent Cade died in 1983, aged 89. But, still now, from May to September, touring companies from around the country perform at the theatre and excited audiences pour in.

www.minack.com

Stay up

The shortest night of the year in the northern hemisphere comes on 21 June: we've been celebrating it for thousands of years now, so you should be able to find a decent party or two. The best place to be, of course, is as far north as possible: in parts of Scotland the sun barely dips below the horizon before it rises again and the night is no longer than a couple of hours. But if you're a druid, Stonehenge is the place to be. About 20,000 people feel that way every year, anyhow.

www.english-heritage.org.uk/server/show/ConWebDoc.15168

Pedal

If you've ever contemplated getting a bit more serious on your bike than just the 20-minute commute to work, this might be the destination for you. Every year at the Bristol Bikefest thousands of large-thighed cyclists gather to compete against each other in three, six, and 12-hour races, then shower (there'll be showers for the first time in 2009 thank God), then lie around and drink and talk about all the bikes they have known before and the bikes they would like to know. It is cyclists' heaven.

www.bike-fest.com

Breathe

There can be no better month to poke around strangers' gardens than June when suddenly everything ripens and swells in luscious summer warmth. All over the country there are open gates to gardens such as Aderyn y môr, ranging along a cliff top in Pembrokeshire, or the four-acre plot at the Bishop's House in Norwich. They fall under various programmes and some, such as those organised by the National Garden Scheme, are raising money for charity all year long while others, such as that in Chipping Campden, take place over just one weekend. It is an amazing chance to see the hard work and love that are poured into these green oases.
www.ngs.org.uk

Celebrate

In the summer of 1969, a group of gay men and women in New York could stand the day-to-day police discrimination no longer and struck back in a series of protests that are now seen as the beginning of the gay rights movement. The following June, the first Gay Pride rally took place to commemorate the Stonewall riots; now the marches happen every year around the world. They're wonderful celebrations, full of glitter and good heart. There's a huge Pride event in London, and more round the country.
www.pridelondon.org; www.oxfordpride.org.uk; www.thanetpride.co.uk; www.brightonpride.org; www.hullpride.com; www.cornwallpride.com; www.swanseapride.com; www.ukblackpride.org.uk

Bibi van der Zee

Summer

Choosing and pitching a tent

Selecting a tent can seem a daunting task given the vast range on offer. To make the process as simple as possible, first consider the reason you want the tent. Is it mainly to stay dry at a rainy festival, for hiking into the hills with a friend or for housing the entire family for two weeks each summer in Cornwall?

Two tents popular with **festival-goers** are the dome and the 'throw-and-go' (or instant tent). The former usually has two bendy poles crisscrossed over one another. It's simple to put up, but can be unstable in high winds. The latter you just toss into the air and it lands fully assembled and ready to peg out. However, taking it down may require a degree in origami and its large, flat disc-shape when packed makes it unwieldy to carry.

Backpackers have quite a spectrum from which to choose. The basic design is the hoop – one arched bendy pole with the flysheet pegged out on either side. Geodesic tents are similar but involve a more complex pole system that makes them more stable (and pricier). Ultralights are usually stripped-down versions of hoop tents –wonderfully light to carry but their specialist materials come at a price. The bivouac (or bivi), meanwhile, is the minimalist's dream – a waterproof cover barely much higher than a person in a sleeping bag, and not one for claustrophobes.

Larger groups are catered for by tunnel tents that are longer and usually taller versions of the hoop tent with two or more arched poles, and frame tents, which tend to be heavy, bulky and often time-consuming to set up, but normally offer separate bedrooms, standing room and a covered common area.

We hope you have many years enjoyment with your tent.

ASSEMBLY INSTRUCTIONS INSIDE

IMPORTANT

Easy to put up, tents are good for keeping dry ... within reason.

Once you have decided the style of tent that best suits you, draw up a checklist by which you can judge each one. Start with the most important feature: how many people does it sleep? Make sure to check the floor size because some two-man tents, in particular, can be very cosy indeed. How heavy and bulky is it? If you're going to be carrying the tent for any distance or popping it into a bicycle pannier, you'll want something light and slimline. Is it waterproof? Some of the cheapest tents are only water-resistant – a subtle but important difference if the skies open at 2am. Does the tent have a flysheet and an inner compartment? Single-skin tents are lighter but prone to condensation. Finally, how big is the porch? Will it be large

enough for your rucksack and boots, and for cooking in bad weather?

Once you have made your choice, make sure you follow the tent's pitching instructions carefully. Here are you few other things you should consider in order to enjoy your camping experience as much as possible.

Pitch your tent where it will be:

- Sheltered, but not under a tree – a branch may fall on you. If there is no shelter, point the side of your tent with the smallest surface area directly into the wind.

- Away from boggy or marshy land or anywhere that may flood.

- Level. If this is not possible, position your tent so that the slope runs head-to-toe rather than side-to-side.

- On ground that is free from holes or bumps. There's nothing like a tree root or a rock in the small of your back for denying you a good night's sleep.

- In a field with no livestock.

- Positioned to catch the sun in the morning. This will warm and dry your tent.

In certain conditions, adhering to one rule may mean breaking another. If so, choose safety over comfort. When the time comes to strike camp, clean and dry your tent as much as possible before you take it down. Before leaving, ensure that anything you may have moved has been replaced and that you take everything with you. Ideally, there should be no sign of your presence, save some flattened grass.

A few more tips:

- Always put up a new tent once (in your garden or local park) before you travel to check you can do it and that all its parts are present and correct.

- Insert pegs pointing inwards at roughly 45 degrees.

- Keep your torch where you can find it easily in the dark.

- In blustery weather, use all your tent's guy-ropes and anchor pegs down with large stones.

- When taking your tent down, use an upside-down peg to pull out any that have become stuck in the ground.

- If you have to pack your tent away wet on your last morning, dry it thoroughly when you get home. This will prevent it being wrecked by mildew.

Dixe Wills

Summer

Predicting the weather

Nothing spoils a day out more quickly than an unexpected drenching. The ability to read the weather yourself could spare you a load of grief and, in extreme conditions, possibly even save your life. There are a variety of means by which you may be able to anticipate what the skies have in store. If you can consult several at the same time and they agree, you'll be well placed to prepare for any changing conditions.

The most obvious indicators of fair or foul weather in the offing are, of course, clouds. Low, dark ones with an anvil-shaped top (cumulonimbus) are precursors of storms, strong winds and, on occasion, hail. Fluffy, cotton-wool clouds (cumulus) promise rain only when numerous and packed close together. High, rippled clouds (cirrocumulus) will soon disperse leaving a clear sky.

The old saying, 'Red sky at night, shepherd's delight. Red sky in morning, shepherd's warning,' has a good deal of sense in it. Red sunsets only occur when there is not much moisture in the air, making it unlikely that it will rain the next day, whereas a red sunrise often heralds a storm.

Missed the sunrise? Check for dew – this forms best at night when there are cloudless skies and little wind about. Therefore, if you encounter no dew on a summer morning, the conditions are ripe for rain.

If you find yourself enjoying a fine, sunny day but the wind suddenly picks up, be on your guard for an imminent change in the weather. Likewise, if you see smoke from a bonfire or chimney that swirls or appears to get knocked down after rising, it is a sign that rain, or possibly a storm, is coming. Conversely, smoke rising in a column signifies fine weather.

It pays to keep your ears open, too. Although it seems unlikely, sound carries further just before it rains, so take note when you become aware of distant noises becoming clearer and sounding louder than normal.

chilling

Sometimes nature prevails, but you can at least be prepared.

Plants and animals, of course, have had to cope with changeable weather for even longer than we have, so it is perhaps not surprising that they have learned to read the signs and react to whatever weather is coming. Here are some of nature's weather forecasters to look out for:

Insect-eating birds

Insects tend to fly lower when rain is due. Although they may be too small to see, you can tell where they are by the behaviour of insect-eating birds such as swallows. If they are flying low in pursuit of food, there is a good chance that rain is imminent.

Cows

When cows are seen to sit down en masse, it is often another sign that rain is on the way. If a storm is due, they also tend to huddle together. It doesn't always work, of course – sometimes cows just need to sit down.

Pine cones

Pine cones open and close depending on levels of humidity. An open cone indicates dry weather, while rain or fog is forecast by a closed cone. More generally, vegetation smells more pungent just before rainfall.

Scarlet pimpernel

An unmistakable wild plant whose flowers – five rounded orange petals with a dash of purple at the centre – can often be found brightening up roadsides. It is also known as the 'shepherd's weatherglass', a weatherglass being a water-based barometer invented in the 17th century. The scarlet pimpernel's flowers close just before bad weather.

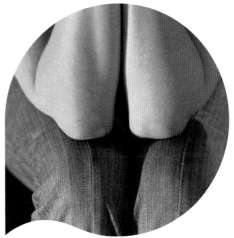

Seaweed

If you are by the seaside and come across bootlace weed (otherwise known as 'mermaid's tresses' – it looks like long, brown hair), hang it up in a sheltered spot. When the humidity is low, the seaweed becomes dry and brittle, meaning it is likely that the next day will be clear.

The human body

Many people claim that they feel arthritic or rheumatic twinges before a cold snap or wet weather. While it is true that arthritis and rheumatism are exacerbated by a drop in temperature, there is no scientific proof that such aches and pains can foretell a cold spell or rain.

Dixe Wills

Fooling a

Brew your own

For most people, the concept of homebrewing goes no further than emptying a packet of Skittles into a bottle of vodka. (Let them steep for a day, then filter and mix with lemonade for a hyperglycaemic treat – but leave out the green ones.) For others, though, homebrewing is practically a religion. Ask any hobby brewer: nothing beats offering a guest your Extra-Special Surprise Ale, then watching their look of unwilling politeness change to one of surprised pleasure as they take a sip and discover it's half decent.

With today's technology, there's a good chance your home-brewed beer will be much better than half decent. As the Craft Brewing Association points out, most commercial bottled ales are pasteurised, taking the edge off the flavour. If you have the right kit, and enough patience, there's no reason you couldn't get real ale at home that tastes as good as the draught ales in country pubs. Plus, over the long run, it can work out much cheaper – 48p a pint for quality real ale from a decent kit, plus around £25 for enough equipment to brew 40 pints – and saves you from queuing up at the beer tent at festivals.

Once the mercury rises, lots of people seeking refreshment turn to cider (or 'zyder' as it is often ironically pronounced, in comedy bad West Country account). This, too, can be made at home, as can perry, which does for pears what ordinary cider does for apples. But purists claim that real cider can only be made with cider apples, washed, sorted, pulped, juiced on a special press and fermented. Some serious machinery is required – a scratter, for pulping, a screw press – and it's not a project to take on lightly.

You can even get a kit that apparently helps you make your own whisky. Although, since it's billed as 'whisky flavour' and has the brand name Prohibition, you have to wonder just how close your finished product would come to the real thing.

Perhaps it's best just to stick to good old-fashioned beer brewing. Of course, this being such a blokey pastime, there are infinite items of specialised kit and ingredients you could potentially acquire in pursuit of your hobby. The instructions

that follow are a simplified version of the simplified method; serious beer-brewers make their own wort (known as "mashing") by extracting sugars from the grain and then boiling it with hops. But they all had to start somewhere, and with a good instruction book and wholesome ingredients, a novice can produce a drink to be proud of – certainly one that beats Skittles-flavoured vodka.

Brewing: A beginner's guide

1. Get together your home-brewing equipment kit. Here's what you need for your first brew: Two 25-litre plastic fermentation bins, a hydrometer, plastic tubing for siphoning, sterilizing chemicals [VWP is the business], and something to put your finished amber nectar in – plastic fizzy pop bottles, large or small, are great for starters as you can't blow them up (unless you're really determined). The rest you can beg, borrow or steal from the kitchen.

2. Buy a 'beer kit', which is basically a tin of wort – that's the term for malt extract that has already been boiled up with hops and concentrated. There's a massive variation in quality and taste between kits, so it's worth going for a good one. By and large they will make 40 pints. Look for a heavier kit (3kg ideally) – the more wort you start off with, the better the end result. You should also get some decent dried yeast – ale or lager yeast depending on what you're brewing. There are kits for all sorts of beer, including ale, stout, pils, wheat beer and more exotic varieties of fruit and honey beer. It goes without saying you should brew something you want to drink!

3. Sterilise all your equipment. Bacteria can really make a mess of your beer. Use a proper sterilising solution (see above), and rinse thoroughly to avoid any off flavours from the solution.

4. Read the instructions on the kit! Follow the volumes closely. The basic method is this – mix your sticky wort with boiling water in one of the fermenting bins – mix thoroughly then top up to the full volume with cold water. If you've followed the volumes correctly, the temperature should be down below 25°C and you can now pitch the yeast. Dried yeast comes with the kit. Save it for priming the bottles and use the proper yeast you bought. Rehydrate it in a sterilized bowl and mix it with your proto-beer. Cover it loosely with the lid, and leave it somewhere reasonably warm. If you've got it right it'll look like what Quatermass met in the pit after a couple of hours. Don't fall in or you'll die (possibly), or throw up (definitely).

5. After two or three days, fermentation should have slowed and the gravity of the wort will have fallen. This means that much of the sugar has turned to alcohol. You can measure this with the hydrometer – sterilise it, drop it in the wort and read it off where it sits in the water – it should now be below 1010.

Siphon your beer off into the other fermentation bin, leaving behind as much yeast as possible. Close the top and leave it for another day to let more yeast settle out.

6. Finally, siphon it back into the cleaned and sterilized other fermentation bin, once again leaving behind as much yeast as possible (your digestive system will thank you for this step, putative home brewers). Clean your bottles, prime them to make the beer slightly fizzy with a tiny amount of the yeast that came with the kit, and half a teaspoon of golden syrup or white sugar per pint. Siphon the beer in to the bottles, leaving a small air gap to help it pressurise. Store upright somewhere cool and enjoy in 3-4 weeks. It'll get better for six months, so don't feel you have to drink it all in the first weekend – no matter how great the temptation.

Stockists / More information

- The Hop Shop, based in Plymouth, supplies just about everything you could possibly want. It comes recommended for its range and low delivery charges (crucial when ordering a 3kg kit).
- Brupaks of Huddersfield are a leading wholesaler of home brew kit and ingredients, and have stockists nationwide.
- There are specialist shops scattered around the UK, too; check craftbrewing.org.uk for a good list. Many, such as The Happy Brewer in Bedford, are staffed by 'brewing fanatics' who can advise on things like spinny sparge arms.
- For bedside reading matter, turn to Graham Wheeler's Brew your own British Real Ale (2009). It's a re-released all-time classic, and available on Amazon or through Camra. Or track down Dave Line's Big Book of Brewing (2004).
- If you're ready to take things further, the Craft Brewing Association has an excellent website, with a selection of recipes and an informative monthly newsletter. Beertools.com, 18000feet.com and jimsbeerkit.co.uk may also prove helpful.
- Camra, the Campaign for Real Ale, has a good website (camra.org.uk) with exhaustive lists of beer festivals (13 in April alone!) and a cider & perry section.
- For cider enthusiasts, ukcider.co.uk has more than 250 pages relating to real cider and perry, including recipes and guides to cobbling together your own equipment from stuff you've found at car boot sales.

Carrie O'Grady and James Weir

Festival People

Rachel Hyde
stilt-walker

I've been a stilt-walker for 20 years. As a kid, I did loads of gymnastics and spent half my life upside down. When I left school, though, I was pushed towards a 'proper' job. I went to art college and worked in graphics for a couple of years, then during the early-90s recession the place where I was working closed down. At the same time, my sister got me some trapeze lessons for a Christmas present and I absolutely loved it.

A bit later I went on a project for unemployed people – which also closed down – but for work experience I had been meant to join the circus. So I rang Zippos and asked, 'Can I still come down?' They said yes. I knew nothing about circuses. I had a Nissan Micra, a dog and a cat. I was supposed to be there for two weeks but stayed two years.

At the beginning I was in the ticket office, but I ended up on trapeze. One of the shows required me to learn stilts. Then my shoulder got really bad from the aerial work – I was having cortisone injections. I wanted to get more grounded, but not that grounded, so switched to stilt-walking. I started making my own costumes and ended up with my own company.

One of my first stilt-walking jobs was at Glastonbury. I loved it – there was always someone to talk to. You get the same comments a lot, mind: 'Aren't you tall? What's the weather like up there? Have you ever fallen over?'

I have only fallen over once, at a show in London. I had a big stilt beast around me with a flame-thrower. Paraffin landed on the floor. I slipped and did the splits. I was shouting, 'Help!', but people thought it was part of the show. I used to do nightclub work, but you get a lot of drunk people trying to push you over.

Sometimes I'll be working and encounter another stilt-walker. There's no rivalry: it's quite nice to see someone your own height.

I do what people ask for, so in recent years I've dressed as a fairy or been sprayed in gold or stood still as a statue. It's full-time and sometimes I work alongside other people, mostly friends. I go where the work is, from corporate-type things to shopping centres. I'm getting more work now than I've ever had. Because of the downturn, shopping centres are putting on entertainment to pull people in and I've had jobs leafleting on stilts. It's so varied and I've never had to supplement it with 'normal' work.

When I joined the circus my parents thought I was absolutely mad and that I'd be back straight away because I would miss my creature comforts. It took them a while to respect what I do, but once they did my mother started proudly saying: 'Oh, my daughter is an artist on trapeze and stilts, you know!'

Loads of my friends are stilt-walkers. It's a way of life, not just work. I get a bit of pain in my shoulder in cold weather, but I really enjoy it. I work everywhere from London to Glasgow, often staying in B&Bs – when I'll hide the stilts in the car. Sometimes I turn up a bit green or something. I've been working as a statue and had to stop for petrol, painted head-to-toe in silver. You get some funny looks.

www.chicksonsticks.co.uk

Dish of the

Black bean and butternut squash thoran

From Big Chill regulars Thali Cafe

Thali Cafe

Serves 4 as a starter, 2 as a main course

Ingredients:
½ butternut squash
2 tbsp vegetable oil
1 tsp white urid dahl
1 tsp black mustard seeds
400ml can cooked black-eyed beans (drained and rinsed)
4 tbsp fresh grated coconut
1 tsp fresh green chilli
1 tsp salt
1 tbsp desiccated coconut
½ tsp turmeric powder
Handful fresh curry leaves

Method:

- Bring a pan of salted water to the boil. Peel the butternut squash, scoop out seeds and pith, and chop half the squash into small cubes – about half-inch square.

- Put the chopped butternut squash in the water and cook for five minutes until the pieces are tender but still have bite. Drain and keep to one side.

- In a large, heavy-based frying pan, heat the vegetable oil until very hot, then add the dahl and black mustard seeds and stir until the dahl starts to brown and the seeds begin to pop and crackle.

- Now add the drained black-eyed beans, cooked butternut squash, salt, green chilli and turmeric powder. Stir thoroughly until the ingredients are really hot and totally covered in the frying spices.

- Now add the fresh coconut, desiccated coconut and curry leaves and fry until all ingredients are equally mixed and sizzling in the pan.

- This thoran is delicious served simply with fresh chapatis, yoghurt and salad.

Drink of th

Summer of love

From the Big Chill bartenders

Mix the grapes, lemon juice and passion fruit syrup in a glass. **Add** the apple juice, vodka and wine then **fill** glass with rocks of ice. **Cover, shake hard** then pour contents into another glass and **top up** with more ice and sauvignon blanc.

10ml lemon juice
5-6 red grapes
10ml passion fruit syrup
5ml sugar syrup
50ml pressed apple
  juice
35ml mango vodka
Sauvignon blanc wine

e month

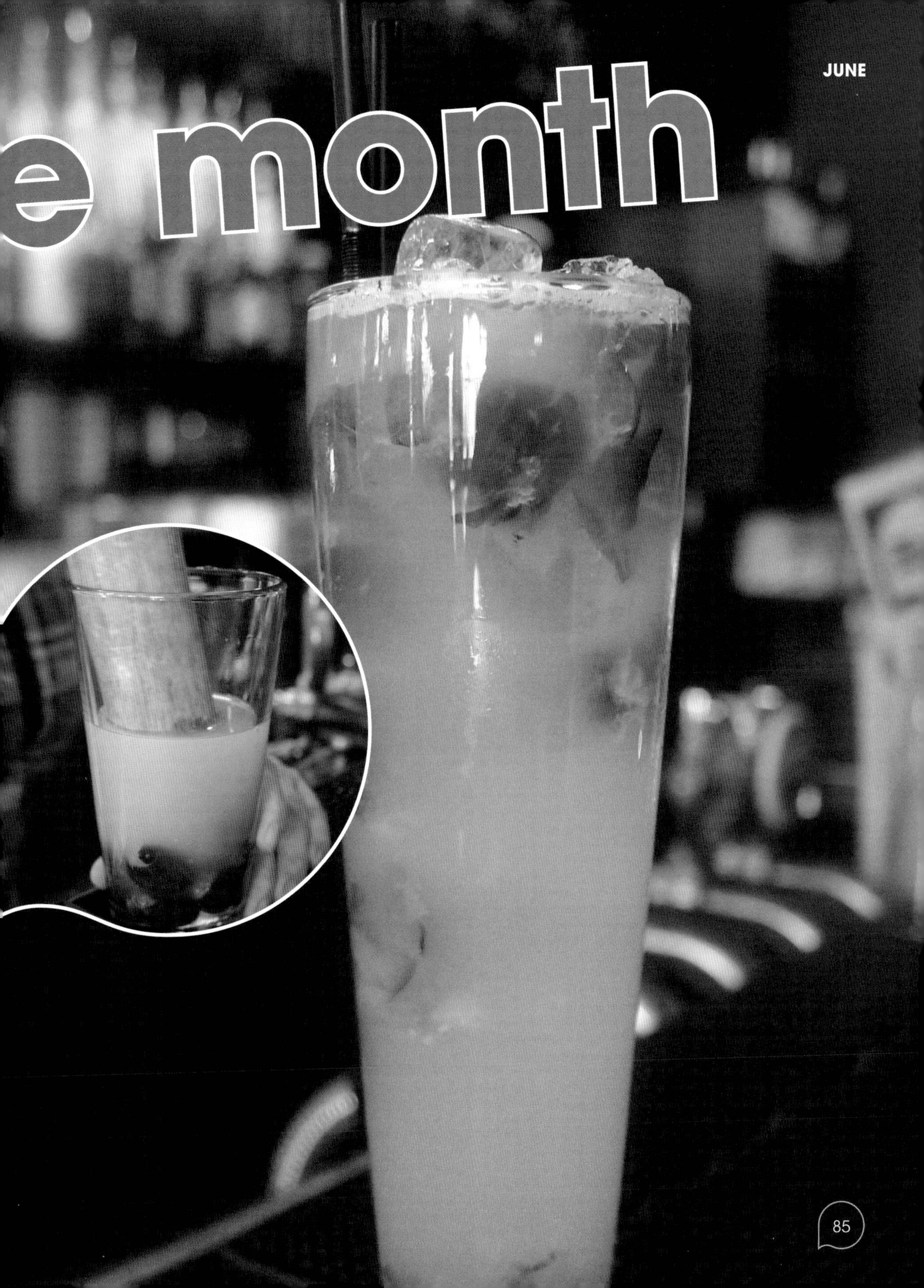

Game of

Toe wrestling

This is as easy to organise as a game of arm wrestling, yet somehow the fact you use another appendage makes it twice as fun.

Toe wrestles are one-on-one, best of three. Contenders sit on the floor facing each other, with one leg each stretched out, big toes linked together. Socks must be removed and, as if we even need to say it, feet should be given a good scrub before battle commences. The only equipment you need is two pieces of string or something similar. Use these to mark out a line about 20cm from either side of the linked feet. The aim of the game is to push your opponent's foot over one of these lines. The non-wrestling foot must be kept off the floor at all times, and part of your bottom must always be on the ground. Make the contest easier by moving the lines closer to the feet, or further away to increase the difficulty. Children and adults can even challenge each other to a match despite their differences in strength – just move one 'score line' closer than the other.

To really get everyone in the mood, why not make up toe-wrestling nicknames for those involved? 'The Toeminator' is one of the frequent winners at the World Toe Wrestling Championships held each year at the Bentley Brook Inn in Derbyshire. The puns don't stop there. You can stage the competition in a 'toedium' and get the referee to announce the battle with the words, 'Toe down'. But what to call out if you want to surrender? 'Toe much!' of course.

Perri Lewis

June festival directory

MUSIC

THE BIG ONES

Download
When: Mid June
Where: Donington Park, Derby, East Midlands
Cost: Weekend adult with camping £160
Website: www.downloadfestival.co.uk
Massive metal and punk festival where it's been known for audiences to throw bottles, bands to throw instruments back and for the riot police to show up. Generally good natured though, if eardrum-bustingly loud.

Glastonbury Festival
When: Late June
Where: Worthy Farm, Glastonbury, Somerset
Cost: Adult weekend around £175
Website: www.glastonburyfestivals.co.uk
The first ever Glasto took place the day after Jimi Hendrix died and cost a pound to get in. Since then a ring of steel has gone up to repel gatecrashers and over 140,000 revellers pay nearly two hundred quid for a ticket. Still the daddy, though.

RockNess
When: Mid June
Where: Clune Farm, Dores, Loch Ness
Cost: Day ticket £35-45. Weekend with camping around £140
Website: www.rockness.co.uk
Don't waste time looking for Nessie. She's not there. Concentrate on the music instead with the likes of Fatboy Slim, Underworld and Orbital creating a beast of a party on the banks of beautiful Loch Ness.

ROCK/INDIE

Beach Break Live
When: Mid June
Where: Polzeath, Cornwall
Cost: Adult around £60-£70
Website: www.beachbreaklive.com
Student high jinks on the Cornish coast – play skittles with your mates in giant Zorbs, try out free-running, enter a dance-off – with headliners like Dizzee Rascal and the Zutons, and just a stone's throw from the beach.

City Showcase
When: Early June
Where: Various venues, London
Cost: £5 for access to all gigs and workshops
Website: www.cityshowcase.co.uk
Tomorrow's talent gets a chance to breakthrough at London's leading showcase for new music and fashion. Organisers lay claim to Amy Winehouse, Lady Sovereign and Keane amongst others. Wannabes are encouraged to apply.

Hard Rock Calling
When: Late June
Where: Hyde Park, London
Cost: Weekend ticket £110, Day ticket £50
Website: www.hardrockcalling.co.uk
Rock royalty – Springsteen, Clapton, the Police, the Who etc – strut their stuff in front of a sea of bald pates and middle aged spreads. You are politely asked not to bring chairs. Rock and roll.

Llama
When: Mid June
Where: Lynton and Lynmouth, Devon
Cost: Free, booking required for some events

Website: www.llama.org.uk

Not-for-profit festival that manages to be laid back, hip and friendly all at the same time. The combo of spectacular coastal setting and names like the legendary Bert Jansch on the bill has quickly turned this into a new favourite.

Middlesbrough Music Live

When: Early June
Where: Centre Square, Middlesbrough
Cost: Free
Website: www.middlesbroughmusiclive. co.uk

Alongside the likes of Ash, the Fratellis and Estelle are a load of bands you won't have heard of yet but probably soon will. Nine stages of breaking talent and all completely free.

Sellindge Music Festival

When: Early June
Where: near Ashford, Kent
Cost: Around £20 a day
Website: www.sellindgemusicfestival.co.uk

The brains behind this one is fulfilling his grandfather's dream of staging a music festival. Grandad must be proud – laid back, inclusive and focused on new music with some big name headliners, this is a promising newbie on the circuit.

Wakestock

When: Late June (Woodstock), Early July (Abersoch)
Where: Woodstock Blenheim Palace, Abersoch Cardigan Bay
Cost: Weekend adult £88.50, Day tickets £44.50
Website: www.wakestock.co.uk

Transforming Cardigan Bay into California for the weekend, wakeboarding is the snowboarding of the watersports world (but you knew that). Dudes skate the water by day and catch acts like Moby, Mark Ronson and the Streets by night.

FOLK

3 Wishes Faery Fest

When: Mid June
Where: Colliford Lake Park, Bodmin Moor, Cornwall
Cost: Adult weekend £85 (£35 day pass), Under 18s £10, Under 12s free (with paying adult)
Website: www.3wishesfaeryfest.co.uk

Not one for the rationalists, expect a lot of very long hair and raggedy hemlines as faerie-loving folk bring their specific brand of fantasy to life in Cornwall. Music, art, workshops and fashion – all of the faery variety.

Beverley Folk Festival

When: Mid June
Where: Beverley, East Yorkshire
Cost: Adult weekend tickets £77 /£58 concession, £212 family (2 adults 2 children)
Website: www.beverleyfestival.com

Quality, friendly folk festival that's been going for twenty-five years, offering the likes of Billy Bragg, Eliza Carthy and Seth Lakeman. Music goes on late into the night and there's a healthy fringe buzzing away in the local boozers.

Big Session Festival

When: Mid June
Where: De Montfort Hall, Leicester
Cost: Adult weekend £60
Website: www.bigsessionfestival.com

Not the wildest party of the summer but a good, grown up vibe which caters to music lovers and their kids, reliably offering a cracking line up – Levellers, Billy Bragg, Ade Edmondson – and solid gold green credentials.

Coastline Bluegrass Festival

When: Early June
Where: Llandudno, Wales
Cost: Weekend with camping around £30
Website: www.coastlinebluegrass.co.uk

American roots music comes to Wales with a festival that aims to teach and entertain. Lovers of the high lonesome sound can catch

The dreaded rain covers of Wimbledon fortnight.

leading bluegrass musicians and attend workshops and picking sessions.

Crawley Folk Festival
When: Late June
Where: The Hawth, Crawley, West Sussex
Cost: Adult weekend around £35
Website: www.myspace.com/crawleyfolkfestival
The idyllic woodland location sets this one apart from the rest. A genuinely eclectic mix of traditional music from English ceilidh bands and Irish bodhran players to Cajun squeezeboxes and Appalachian pickers.

Dent Folk Festival
When: Late June
Where: Buck Bank Farm, Under the Howgill Fells, near Sedbergh, Cumbria
Cost: Around £50
Website: www.dentfolkfestival.co.uk
An all rounder of a folk festie that's outgrown its original site and moved to a new venue in the spectacular Yorkshire Dales, expect theatre, crafts, circus skills workshops, puppet shows and plenty of live music and dancing.

Southwell Folk Festival
When: Early June
Where: The Southwell Workhouse, Southwell, nr Nottingham
Cost: Adults around £50, Children £20 (12-17), Family ticket £110
Website: www.southwellfolkfestiva.org.uk
Serving up the holy trinity of folk festivals (that's music, dancing and drinking of course) this one kicks off with a twelve mile Morris dance relay and is supported by a beer festival showcasing over forty microbrewery beers.

Kingsbridge Music Festival
When: Mid June
Where: Kingsbridge town centre, various venues
Cost: Some free some small charge events
Website: www.kingsbridgemusicfest.co.uk
An exuberant little festival where organisers just want it to be fun and exhort you to 'get your ears on'! Acts are mainly from the South West with a smattering of bigger names, all performing in the bandstand on the Quay.

Leamington Peace Festival
When: Mid June
Where: Leamington Spa, Warwickshire
Cost: Free
Website: www.peacefestival.org.uk
Born when hippies were first invented and still going strong thirty odd years later, this is a gentle hand knitted festival of craft stalls, workshops, campaign info, local art, healers and jolly nice people.

Leigh Folk Festival
When: Late June
Where: Leigh-on-Sea, Essex
Cost: Mostly free, small charge for some events
Website: www.leighfolkfestival.co.uk
Hundreds of bands, thousands of revellers and all kinds of dancing. Strut your stuff at the barn dance or flex your vocal chords at the numerous singarounds and open mic competitions.

Raglan Music Festival
When: Mid June
Where: Raglan, Monmouthshire
Cost: Events individually price between Free-£10
Website: www.raglan-festival.org
Over forty gigs plus jam sessions in the pub open to all. Clearly speaking from painful experience organisers politely remind you to tune your instrument before you start and to perform songs you actually know. Ouch.

Strawberry Fair
When: Early June
Where: Cambridge, Cambridgeshire
Cost: Free
Website: www.strawberry-fair.org.uk
Loll about in the summer sunshine at a real old-fashioned fair. Run by enthusiastic volunteers in aid of local charities, there's a laid back mix of live music, arts and crafts over two days.

Togfest
When: Late June
Where: Bradwell Abbey, Milton Keynes, Buckinghamshire
Cost: See website
Website: www.togfest.org
Strictly limited to 2,000 to keep things friendly and intimate, this is a hassle-free, family friendly zone with great music and lots of extra curricular activity to keep everyone entertained.

Wimborne Folk Festival
When: Mid June
Where: Wimborne, Dorset
Cost: Adult weekend £68 (with camping £76)
Website: www.wimbornefolkfestival.co.uk
Join 30,000 other folk enthusiasts who take over picturesque Wimborne for one weekend every June. Risk whiplash at a ceilidh, watch feet fly at one of the dance displays or just sup beer to the strains of live folk music.

Wirral Folk on the Coast
When: Early June
Where: The OC Club, Bridle Road, Bromborough, Wirral
Cost: Adult weekend around £50-£60
Website: www.wirralfolkonthecoast.com
A traditional line up of craft stalls, food, beer, live music, workshops and sing-alongs. Bring your instruments and join in the fun.

DANCE/ELECTRONICA

Coloursfest
When: Early June
Where: Braehead Arena and Waterfront, Glasgow
Cost: Adults £42
Website: www.colours.co.uk
Herds of excited clubbers head for six arenas of organ-rattling dance music held, somewhat incongruously, next door to a shopping mall. Weather-proofed dance fest with headliners such as Sasha, Sister Bliss and Carl Cox.

Escape Into the Park
When: Mid June
Where: Singleton Park, Swansea
Cost: Adult £45
Website: www.escapefestival.com
Top up your spray tan, pack your whistle and cram on to one of the free shuttle buses heading for the biggest date on the Welsh dance calendar where you can wave your glowsticks to the likes of Underworld, Judge Jules and Eric Prydz.

CLASSICAL

Aldeburgh Festival
When: Mid/Late June
Where: Snape Maltings, nr Aldeburgh, Suffolk
Cost: Events individually priced
Website: www.aldeburgh.co.uk
Specialising in new or forgotten music, fresh interpretations of classical repetoire and building long term relationships with artists. All of impeccable quality, as you'd expect from a festival founded by Benjamin Britten.

Bath International Music Festival
When: Late May/Early June
Where: Locations throughout Bath
Cost: Events individually priced
Website: www.bathmusicfest.org.uk
Started just after World War II this has a line up and reputation only rivalled by the very best international festivals. Top orchestras, ground breaking cross genre collaborations and virtuoso performances, this is high calibre stuff.

Glasgow International Jazz Festival
When: Mid/Late June
Where: Mainly Glasgow's major concert hall and Carling Academy, plus the Tron Theatre
Cost: Events individually priced
Website: www.jazzfest.co.uk
Jazz-sceptics, prepare to be converted. From trombone blasting trad, swing, late night jazz joints and paddlesteamer cruises to wonky jazz-rock and punk-influenced jazz, there will be something here you can dig, man.

Hampton Court Palace Festival

When: Early/Mid June
Where: Hampton Court Palace, Surrey
Cost: Events individually priced from £40–£150
Website: www.hamptoncourtfestival.com

Legendary acts in a venue positively singing with romantic, bloody history. Have a picnic in the 17th century gardens and then catch the likes of Katherine Jenkins, Van Morrison or Rufus Wainwright on the dramatic courtyard stage.

London International Music Show

When: Mid June
Where: ExCeL exhibition centre, London Docklands, Greater London
Cost: See website
Website: www.londoninternationalmusicshow.com

The big draw here is less the live music and more the seminars, free tuition, careers fair, instrument demos, product launches, clinics, masterclasses and hundreds of trade stalls. Muso heaven.

St Magnus Festival

When: Mid/Late June
Where: St Magnus, Orkney Islands
Cost: See website
Website: www.stmagnusfestival.com

A truly unique pairing – the cream of the international music scene and the magic of Orkney – that rewards those prepared to travel for their cultural kicks. The festival overlaps with highly regarded composing and conducting courses.

INTERNATIONAL

Hove

When: Late June
Where: Arendal, Norway
Cost: 5 day pass 230 euros
Website: www.hovefestivalen.com

Fresh new face on the circuit offering line-ups to rival any of the establishd biggies – Gossip, Amy Winehouse, the Ting Tings – located on flawless Norwegian island. So pick up your litter or be shunned.

Hampton Court Palace – not just history and ghosts.

Rock am Ring

When: Early June
Where: Nurburgring racetrack in Nurburg, Germany
Cost: Around £135
Website: www.rockamring.co.uk
Big German rock fest with the likes of Marilyn Manson, Slipknot, Red Hot Chilli Peppers and Rage Against the Machine performing to (we're guessing) a sea of black leather and furry armpits.

Sonar

When: Mid/Late June
Where: Barcelona, Spain, various venues
Cost: Weekend 140 euros. Day pass 30 euros
Website: www.sonar.es
An antidote to the more mainstream festivals on the circuit, this is an avant garde mash up of dance music, film and video that offers more of a challenge for the ears. And you get a chance to top up your tan.

Southside & Hurricane

When: Mid June
Where: Scheeßel, Lower Saxony (Hurricane) and Neuhausen, nr Stuttgart (Southside)
Cost: Adult weekend 110 euros
Website: www.getgo.de; www.hurricane.de; www.southside.de
Twin festivals in the north and south on the same weekend that share largely the same line up – Nick Cave, Franz Ferdinand, Radiohead etc. This is Germany, so expect super organised camping and lots of top quality beer.

ARTS

Ashbourne Festival

When: Mid June/Early July
Where: Ashbourne, Derbyshire
Cost: Events individually priced, some free
Website: www.ashbournefestival.co.uk
Another eclectic mix of high arts (opera, classical music) and street performance, theatre, talks and craft stalls, taking over the small market town of Ashbourne for two weeks every summer.

Chichester Festivities

When: Late June/Early July
Where: Venues around Chichester
Cost: Events individually priced
Website: www.chifest.org.uk
A real mixed bag of recitals, high-minded talks and concerts in the cathedral alongside dramatic street art, parades and populist offerings like Abba tribute bands and big bang firework displays.

Coin Street Festival

When: June/July
Where: Bernie Spain Wharf, London
Cost: Free
Website: www.coinstreet.org/coinstreet_festival.aspx
Have a blast and get to feel all warm and fuzzy inside at the same time. This series of free events is run by a social enterprise and development trust that aims to make London's South Bank a better place for all.

Corsham Festival

When: End June
Where: Around Corsham Village, Wiltshire
Cost: Events individually priced
Website: www.corshamfestival.blogspot.com
One for the discerning music lover, this has developed a reputation for programming new work by emerging and established British composers and takes place in an absurdly picturesque Cotswolds market town.

Grassington Festival

When: Mid June/Early July
Where: Grassington, Yorkshire
Cost: Events individually priced
Website: www.grassington-festival.org.uk
Film nights, art installations, popular jazz, folk, gospel and classical music, celebrity appearances, workshops, comedy, theatre, oh and local crafts like dry stone walling. So, a bit of everything then.

Greenwich and Docklands International Festival

When: Mid June
Where: Venues in Greenwich and Docklands

A world of wood awaits at Woodfest Wales. Saw on!

Cost: Events individually priced, much free
Website: www.festival.org
A festival dedicated to outdoor arts, expect jaw-dropping feats of acrobatics, death-defying dance (you just know overhead tango will be gorgeous) and eye-popping pyrotechnics.

Hebden Bridge Arts Festival
When: Late June/Early July
Where: Various locations in the Calder Valley and area surrounding Hebden Bridge
Cost: Events individually priced
Website: www.hebdenbridge.co.uk
Multi-arts festival that offers everything from belly laughs with Phill Jupitus to recitals in the parish church, Samuel Beckett plays to audiences with Nicholas Parsons. Take your pick.

Ludlow Festival
When: End June/Early July
Where: Castle Square, Ludlow, Shropshire
Cost: See website
Website: www.ludlowfestival.co.uk
A summer institution for Shropshire folk, this has been going for fifty years and offers a reliable mix of Shakespeare, opera, classical music, heritage walks and talks from the likes of Derek Jacobi and David Frost.

Watch This Space Festival
When: June/July
Where: Outside the National Theatre
Cost: Events priced individually
Website: www.nationaltheatre.org.uk
Your eyes do not deceive you. That giant AstroTurf three-piece suite is the venue for the National Theatre's free festival of al fresco theatre, dance and circus. Fingers crossed for sunshine or the furniture will be ruined.

Woodfest Wales
When: Early June
Where: St. Asaph, North Wales
Cost: Adults around £8; concessions £7, children £2. Camping for two adults £30
Website: www.woodfestwales.co.uk
Who knew wood could be so much fun? Chainsaw carving, pole climbing, wood chopping contests (grrr), lots of heavy machinery and tools on sale, ooh and displays of teeny tiny little bonsai trees.

LITERATURE/WRITTEN WORD

Borders Book Festival
When: Mid June
Where: Harmony Garden, Melrose
Cost: Events individually priced

Website: www.bordersbookfestival.org
Quickly established as one of the UK's
premier literary events expect big names
– Michael Palin, Germaine Greer, Rory
Bremner, Alistair Campbell – and unusual
venues like ruined abbeys and tranquil
gardens.

Broadstairs Dickens Festival
When: Late June
Where: Venues throughout Broadstairs
Cost: Events individually priced
Website: www.broadstairsdickensfestival.
co.uk
Fabulously costumed locals get right into the
Dickensian spirit of things to transform the
town into a Victorian holiday resort. Enjoy
melodramas on the seafront, bathing parties,
music hall entertainments and a traditional
street fair.

Humber Mouth: Hull Literature Festival
When: Late June/Early July
Where: Hull Central Library and other
venues around the city
Cost: Events individually priced, some free
Website: www.humbermouth.org.uk
A literary festival with a bit of urban grit,
how-to events are mixed up with activities
for children and big name author talks from
the likes of John Pilger, Susie Orbach, Russel T
Davies and Joan Bakewell.

Lowdham Book Festival
When: Late June
Where: Lowdham village and Broadway
Cinema, Nottingham
Cost: Events individually priced
Website: www.lowdhambookfestival.co.uk
A week of bookish delights in the tiny
village of Lowdham where budding writers
and dedicated book lovers can enjoy author
talks, a book fair and lots of events for
children.

Stratford Upon Avon Poetry Festival
When: June/July, events throughout
Where: Shakespeare Centre and
Shakespeare Institute, Stratford Upon Avon

Cost: Free- £15, concessions £2 less
Website: www.shakespeare.org.uk
For those of a poetic persuasion, get some
inspiration in the ludicrously picturesque
town of Shakespeare's birth. Professional and
amateur poets get together to exchange
words and ideas.

OUTDOORS

Bristol Bike Festival
When: Early June
Where: Ashton Court, Bristol
Cost: Race entry £30 per team of riders
Website: www.bike-fest.com
Bike racing for experienced and novice riders
over a 10k looped track set up for two days of
solo, pairs and team events. If you're not stiff
as board afterwards there's live music and
partying.

Chap & Hendrick's Olympics
When: Late June/Early July
Where: Bedford Square, London
Cost: Free
Website: www.hendricksgin.com
A gin-soaked sports day of the absurd,
games commence with the lighting of the
pipe and an amble round the gardens,
winners do a victory sashay and events
include Neck-tie Kwon Do and Bounders.
Very, very silly.

Wimbledon Tennis Championships
When: Late June/Early July
Where: Wimbledon, London
Cost: Depending on match and time, pay
between £5–£100
Website: www.wimbledon.org
No more Cliff Richard moments now
Centre Court has a retractable roof but
still the quintessential English day out. Eat
exorbitantly-priced strawberries in the rain,
get a bit squiffy on Pimms and big up the
Brits on court.

World Naked Bike Ride
When: Early/Mid June
Where: Hyde Park, London

Cost: Free
Website: www.worldnakedbikeride.org
Forget the sunscreen at your peril and maybe avert your eyes from the riders ahead when you're going uphill. Naked cycling in protest against global oil dependency is serious fun, especially for the spectators. Go as bare as you dare.

ALTERNATIVE ENTERTAINMENT

Biggin Hill Air Show
When: End June
Where: Biggin Hill Airport, Kent
Cost: Adult, £21 child £7
Website: www.bigginhillairfair.co.uk
Come over all nostalgic amongst the Spitfires, Hurricanes and Lancasters and get a crick in your neck goggling at death-defying aerial acrobatics. Held at the legendary RAF airfield.

Cheltenham Science Festival
When: Early June
Where: Cheltenham, Gloucestershire
Cost: See website
Website: www.cheltenhamfestivals.com/science
Fire up your Bunsen burners and prepare to find science fun. Yes, fun. Demos that will boggle your kids' brains (and yours) plus grown up talks and workshops that explain what the boffins have discovered recently.

Pride London
When: Late June/Early July
Where: Parade from Oxford Street to Victoria Embankment, party nucleus around Soho
Cost: Events individually priced, much free
Website: www.pridelondon.org
One in the eye for the bigots, is there a parade more colourful, outrageous and downright joyful than pride? Two weeks of art, debate and performance culminate in a procession like no other.

Rose Week
When: Mid June
Where: Sudeley Castle Gardens, Winchcombe, Gloucestershire
Cost: Castle entry £7.20, concessions apply and children under 5 go free

Chocks away at the thrilling Biggin Hill Air Show.

Celebrate your inner 'Fabulous' at Pride London.

Website: www.sudeleycastle.co.uk
Literally a chance to stop and smell the roses – hundreds of them. Take a gentle amble through the castle grounds and talk to experts and gardeners. Blooming marvellous.

Stonehenge Solstice Celebration
When: Summer Solstice
Where: Stonehenge, Wiltshire
Cost: Free if arriving at certain times
Website: www.new-age.co.uk
No longer a somewhat surreal battleground between druids, hippies and the police, nowadays English Heritage lets people into Stonehenge to see the sunrise on the start of summer. Still strictly no clambering about on the stones, obviously.

World Nettle Eating Competition
When: Mid/Late June
Where: The Bottle Inn, Marshwood, Dorset
Cost: Free or nominal charge for entry
Website: www.thebottleinn.co.uk
Like many of life's greatest pleasures, this started out as a (presumably drunken) conversation in the pub and has morphed into a proper contest with rules and everything. They make their own fun in Dorset, you know.

FOOD & DRINK

BBC Summer Good Food Show
When: Early June
Where: The NEC, Birmingham
Cost: Adult day ticket is £18.50
Website: www.bbcgoodfoodshowsummer.com
In the massive hangar-like space that is the NEC you'll find packs of celeb chefs dishing up masterclasses, never-ending lines of food stalls and absolutely masses of food to eat.

Cheltenham Food and Drink Festival
When: Mid June
Where: Montpelier Gardens, Cheltenham
Cost: £5 adults
Website: www.garden-events.com

Like the best kind of garden party, sip champagne/real ale/local cider to the sound of live jazz, soak up the sun (hopefully) and eat stupid amounts of food. Over 150 local artisans peddle their wares.

Flavour of Shetland
When: End June
Where: Lerwick, Shetland
Cost: Nominal entry fee, many free events
Website: www.flavourofshetland.com
The flavour in this case isn't confined just to food and drink, although there's plenty of it. You also get traditional Shetland culture, crafts and music, and over 40,000 intrepid festival goers who've made it a long way north to join in.

Taste of London
When: June
Where: Regent's Park, London
Cost: Events are variously priced
Website: Review at www.channel4.com/life/microsites/T/taste2008
Like a massive picnic in the park except you don't have to bother packing the basket – the best restaurants in London are bringing the food and wine. Just stock up on the festival currency and get sampling.

Emma McGowan

july

'The only place I can really be me' – Norman Jay

illustration Sarah King

Wiltshire

www.womad.org/festivals/charlton-park

Whether it's Mbiran thumb piano, Uzbekistani opera, Celtic 'acid croft' beats, Japanese aboriginal dub or, er, Rolf Harris on wobble-board, WOMAD is the one festival that can genuinely say it's got something for even the most obscure tastes. And that goes for people who snort at the term 'world music', too. WOMAD – World of Music, Art and Dance – may have brought the genre into the public eye, but the festival goes far beyond the stereotype of exotic women wailing in a foreign language over a western drum beat. A few years ago, you could have heard a Trinidadian steel band tackle Offenbach while, over on another stage, Robert Plant belted out Black Dog. Talk about a global village.

WOMAD was founded in 1982 by musician Thomas Brooman, journalist Bob Hooton and Peter Gabriel, who was reportedly struck by inspiration when, spinning his radio dial in search of Radio 4, he chanced on a Dutch station that was playing African music. The first festival saw Echo & the Bunnymen joined on stage by the Drummers of Burundi, much to the audience's delight. It was the sort of serendipitous cross-cultural hookup that would become characteristic of WOMAD. Ian McCulloch later recalled: 'We asked them to do it because we'd seen them in some field playing, and they were fantastic. It was mad. They didn't speak English – Pete [De Freitas] kind of led them through it.' Brooman, for his part, recalls being first frightened that the pop fans would boo the drummers off stage, then delighted at the crowd's 'rapturous response'.

Whatever your plumage, all tribes are welcome at WOMAD.

Since then, WOMAD has grown into a full-fledged multicultural blowout, with musicians pitching in between gigs to lead workshops for festivalgoers – teaching them everything from Iraqi classical song to windsock-making (because you never know when you might need a windsock). Kids in particular are well catered for, in every sense: there are plenty of opportunities for Scandinavian sweets in between bouts of bamboo nose flute-making. The bazaar, too, goes one step beyond the usual rag-tag line of stalls selling bongs and hemp rucksacks; at WOMAD, you can expect a rag-tag line of stalls selling bongs, hemp rucksacks, Moroccan lanterns, Mexican jewellery and every conceivable variety of hand-drum.

The performers themselves, by all accounts, have a ball. Many are strangers to the us-and-them mentality of pampered UK artists,

page 106 ▶

THE BIGCHILL recommends

The Secret Garden Party

Secret location, East Anglia

www.secretgardenparty.com

Want to see how the other half live? Then the Secret Garden Party is for you. The festival was the brainchild of a capital young chap named Freddie Fellowes, heir to the 4th Baron de Ramsey, and takes place on some of the family's 6,000-acre chunk of Cambridgeshire. Plenty of Freddie's friends turn up for what would undoubtedly be called Poshstock if some other festival hadn't already nicked the name.

There's no snootiness at the Secret Garden party, though. Artists' VIP areas are banned, so they must mingle with the crowd, and the atmosphere is very much one of unabashed and uniquely English upper-crust silliness. Punters can amuse themselves with snail races, sock wrestling tournaments, mass waltzes, human Tetris or that simple yet satisfying favourite, the pillow fight. Dressing-up is popular, with fairy wings and tutus taking pride of place.

Of course, there are bands, too; 2008 was notable for hosting the only UK performance by Grace Jones. (It was abruptly cut short by Fellowes when she overran her slot – brave lad!). You don't go here for the bands, though, as Fellowes has freely admitted: 'We aim the event towards getting as many people to meet as possible. What you remember about a party is the people you meet. That's where the magic is, not seeing the most amazing band in the world.'

Certainly, this festival has a magic all its own. The DJ booth is particularly special; its home is on a large wooden jetty on the shores of the beautiful lake, so you feel you could be dancing right on the water, which makes a change from the usual sweaty tent full of shreds of dead grass. The lake is the centrepiece of the whole show, hosting sport (boat races – jolly good show, chaps!) and theatre (a burning pirate ship), as well as providing a good spot for fizzy-headed punters to zone out and watch the ducks. Food is fancy, and cocktails are popular. Tea, as you might expect, sells well.

Fellowes used money left to him by his grandfather to fund the first Secret Garden Party in 2004, and avoids corporate sponsorship. When he comes into the baronetcy, he will reportedly inherit £35m. The mind boggles to think what sort of a party he could put on with that.

Carrie O'Grady

so there's not so much cowering in the VIP area. In 2007, the year of 'Womud', musicians from the drier parts of the world could be seen struggling to walk in borrowed English wellies – and taking each other's photographs with glee.

With the emphasis so much on diversity, it's said the best way to see the best bands at WOMAD is just to wander through the famous forest of silk flags until you hear something you like. It might be Youssou N'Dour; it might be an old Loop Guru track in the Whirl-Y-Gig dance tent; it might be a chartered accountant having his first go on the bongos. The smaller tents, notably the one sponsored by Radio 3, are well worth keeping an eye on: their more intimate acoustic is better suited to much of this sort of music, and they're more likely to provide happy discoveries. But wherever you go, keep an eye out among the henna'ed hordes for a celebrity or two waving an Amnesty petition, or the Earl and Countess of Suffolk, owners of the ground, and their cronies. One festivalgoer reports hearing a well-heeled visitor trilling into her mobile, as the strains of Eddy Grant's Electric Avenue wafted across the field: 'Oh yes, it's a lovely event, and that Eddie Murphy's on stage tonight!'

Carrie O'Grady

Sticking around

Malmesbury and Wiltshire

The eclectic sounds of Womad will probably leave you in that marvellous state of feeling both chilled and invigorated, so if you can take a few days out afterwards, you're in the perfect place to explore Wiltshire. Much of the county is designated as an Outstanding Area of Natural Beauty and dotted with sites of prehistoric interest.

WHERE TO CAMP

The campsite at Stowford Manor Farm, Wingfield, lies in a beautiful setting with the River Frome on one side and medieval farmhouse buildings on the other. It has only a small number of pitches with room to breathe between them, so campers won't feel crowded. The farm also runs a range of workshops including stone and marble masonry, photography and sculpture.
www.stowfordmanorfarm.co.uk

Centrally located near Devizes, the Bell Caravan and Camping Park is a great base to explore Wiltshire's attractions, from nearby Stonehenge to Salisbury. The pitches back on to fields so there is plenty of space to stretch your legs as you take in views across the vale. Facilities include an outdoor pool and barbecue area.
www.caravancampingsites.co.uk/
wiltshire/thebell.htm

WHAT TO DO

Walking

With more than 7,500 walking paths, there's no better way to see Wiltshire than on foot. There are famous National Trails such as the 139km Ridgeway, a neolithic trade route. Starting in the World Heritage Site of Avebury, it will take you past many prehistoric sites including the Avebury Stone Circle, (which, unlike Stonehenge, you can walk through and touch) the Hackpen Horse chalk cutting (one of many in Wiltshire), and Silbury Hill, a 40-metre man-made mound, the purpose of which remains a mystery.
www.nationaltrail.co.uk/Ridgeway

A walk on the Salisbury Plain is also a good choice, offering spectacular views.
www.visitwiltshire.co.uk/site/things-to-do/activities/walking

Swimming

Farleigh and District Swimming club (situated just downstream from the Stowford Manor campsite) is the only river swimming club remaining in the country. Kick back in unbeatable surrounds, then sun yourself in the bathing area. Toilets, changing rooms and parking available. £1 per swim or £10 for yearly membership.
www.stowfordmanorfarm.co.uk

Wild spot

The Vaughan-Pickard Nature Reserve on Blackmoor Copse, six miles east of Salisbury, is a stunning spot known for some of the rarest butterflies in the UK, such as the pearl-bordered fritillary. There's an hour-long circular walk on which you might see dormice, great-crested newts and woodcock, along with some big, old spreading ash and oak trees.
www.wiltshirewildlifetrust.org.uk

We dare you

Skydiving is always good for a dare, and with the Tandom Jump team at Netheravon you can take a tandem or solo leap – extensive training included. Something to cross off your '50 things to do before I die' list or make it the first step in becoming a qualified skydiver.
www.tandemjump.co.uk

... or you could be watching the telly.

If it rains

Try the Atwell-Wilson Motor Museum at Calne, east of Chippenham, where you can see an impressive collection of rare cars from a 1938 Daimler to a 1961 Plymouth Fury. If two wheels are more your thing, there's a 1970 Triumph Bonneville and a 1961 Velocette.
www.atwellwilson.org.uk

If motors aren't your thing, then you can't go wrong with a cathedral, and Salisbury Cathedral is one of the most imposing you'll come across. The medieval monument is a centre of pilgrimage for hundreds of thousands of people every year. You can climb Britain's highest spire or maybe just catch a choral evensong.
www.salisburycathedral.org.uk

FOOD AND DRINK

Beer

Arkell's brewery in Swindon is famous throughout the land and is still making beer in much the same way as John Arkell did when he started in 1843. It produces loads of different brews, including seasonal ones – you'll have to try the summer ale – which are available at the brewery's many Wiltshire pubs.
www.arkells.com

Wine

A' Beckett's Vineyard at Littleton Panell, near Devizes, has nearly five hectares (12 acres) planted with both vines and orchards and is developing a range of wines and ciders that are vegan-friendly.

Get your pagan on – Stonehenge awaits …

Tours and tastings can be arranged for a small fee. Their tipples have so far won silver and bronze medals at the English and Welsh Wine of the Year awards in 2008 and 2007.

www.abecketts.co.uk

Local produce

You can't mention Wiltshire without thinking pig. Famous for ham and pork products, local traditional treats like the Lardy Pie and Bacon Fraise (a fattening breakfast for 15th-century field workers consisting of fried bacon covered in egg batter then baked) wouldn't exist without the county's long association with swine. Farmers' markets abound in Wiltshire and you'll find one near you selling the best local produce, including some mean chutneys to go with your ham and all sorts of other goodies.

www.wiltshirefarmersmarkets.org.uk

FOR THE KIDS

For an animal reserve with a difference, take the kids to Bush Farm and Bison Centre at West Knoyle. They will gawp at the big, shaggy creatures, while the raccoons, prairie dogs and chipmunks might bring back memories of Little House of the Prairie for those of a certain age among the adults. There is also an exhibit of North American artifacts and you can buy bison and elk meat in the shop (but you might not want to tell the kids that).

www.bisonfarm.co.uk

If your kids are avid viewers of BBC's Animal Park, then Longleat will already be on your Wiltshire itinerary. The safari park is situated near Warminster. A tour will take you through tiger territory, lion country, past the pelican pond, into the monkey jungle, then the big game reserve, and you're likely to see many, many other furry, fluffy and growling attractions along the way. There are lots of educational and conservation activities available too, and other sights include one of Britain's grandest Elizabethan stately homes and a hedge maze made from 16,000 English yews.

www.longleat.co.uk

july

Make the most of the month

Pedal

Sometimes it's good to see your own country through a visitor's eyes: the Fat Tire Bike Tour of London is a gentle pedal around the highlights of our capital that we so often forget. It's a four-hour trip, mostly through the royal parks (you're only on streets for less than 12 minutes) and it's very, very easy-going. There aren't a lot of big hills in the centre of town. The route takes you past Big Ben, the Houses of Parliament, Buckingham Palace, Westminster Abbey, Hyde Park Corner and the Princess Diana memorial. It would be interesting to meet any Londoner who has actually visited any of these sites recently ...
www.fattirebiketours.com/london

Bite

No summer is complete without a new food discovery and St George's market in Belfast is a wonderful place to start looking. You can taste fish landed at Portavogie, beef from Armagh and organic fruit and vegetables from Culdrum and Millbrook farms. The coffee is good and there's often a musician or two, which makes it a pretty glorious way to spend a Saturday morning. The market runs every Friday and Saturday and it's one of the most vibrant and enjoyable in the UK.
www.belfastcity.gov.uk/stgeorgesmarket/

Plough

There is something surprisingly wonderful about vintage steam tractors. Just like the titanic shire horses who used to work our farms, steam tractors have strength and beauty that remind us of other times. They are built along completely different lines from modern machinery – to last and last and last. At the Cumbria Steam Gathering, which has been going since the 1970s, thousands of enthusiasts gather every year to admire these impressive beasts. Other highlights include the Wall of Death and a host of classic cars.
www.steamgathering.org.uk

Battle

There were so many battles and struggles in the long, long Wars of the Roses that it is hard to know why the Battle of Tewkesbury in 1471 stands out. Some claim it as the last battle of the wars, but the disputes over the succession to the English throne – as documented in Shakespeare's history plays – would continue for another 16 years. It is Tewkesbury, however, that is commemorated every year in one of Europe's largest re-enactments: thousands take part and thousands come to watch. If you've never seen a re-enactment before, this is the one to start with.
www.tewkesburymedievalfestival.org

Get wet

If you still pine for Daniel Day-Lewis in The Last of the Mohicans when he passionately tells his love, 'I will find yooo! No matter what occurs!' before leaping into a waterfall, this could be your chance to recreate that moment. Just set off along the Four Waterfalls walk in the Brecon Beacons where two rivers – the Hepste and the Mellte – tumble their way down cliffs and through an underground cave. One waterfall in particular, the Sgwd Yr Eira, has a path behind it you can carefully follow – probably best not to jump through on second thoughts (this is Wales, not Hollywood). The flow of the waterfall varies, depending on recent rainfall, from a gentle trickle to a soak-you-to-the-skin gush. It's a bit of a scramble at points, but exhilarating.
www.walkscene.co.uk/Wales/Brecons/Waterfall1.htm

Care

More respect for the wonders of the insect world is what we need. As our bee and insect populations show signs of decline, conservationists are urging us to do everything we can to help by creating habitats – such as ponds, wild areas, wood piles, compost heaps and hedgerow – where possible in our gardens. The city of York has even gone to the extent of holding an insect festival that will bring together local natural history societies and exhibitors, and include lectures and demonstrations. It's going to be buzzing.
www.royensoc.co.uk

Beachcomb

The only way to make absolutely sure you aren't wasting your life is to spend a warm summer's evening wandering a beach in search of driftwood, shells and the remains of strange sea creatures. If you want to do it somewhere special, try Runswick Bay, just north of Whitby in Yorkshire, which has been voted England's best beach for beachcombing. This part of our coastline is known as the Dinosaur Coast and the pools on the beach are full of fossils. The sand is golden and soft between your toes, and there's a pint of good Yorkshire ale available at the nearby Royal Hotel.
www.runswick.com

Clamber

In 2008 Honister Slate Mine opened the UK's first via ferrata – a terrifying and thrilling web of steel ladders and bridges up to the summit of Fleetwith Pike in the Lake District. This is the route that miners in the area used to take to work; it makes the average commute look like a stroll to the corner shop. The idea of the via ferrata originated in Italy and is common on the continent: it makes climbing safer and easier. If heights are your thing, there's no way you can resist this. The mine owners also have nearby cottages that are available to rent.
www.honister-slate-mine.co.uk

Strum

So you've been practising Stairway to Heaven on your guitar for three years now and are beginning to think you'll never get past the intro. Perhaps this is the moment to get a bit more serious with a guitar-playing weekend. At the beautiful Cricket St Thomas in Somerset (run by Warner Leisure Hotels), you'll have two two-hour sessions on an electric guitar. Teacher Graham Barnes admits that he can't get you to Hendrix level in two days, but 'you'd be amazed how much you can learn in just a few hours'.
www.warnerleisurehotels.co.uk

Cheer

Every year since 1715, the watermen of the Thames have raced their single sculls from London Bridge to Chelsea. It's the oldest continuous sporting event in the UK and probably one of the oldest in the world. Thomas Doggett, an Irish theatre manager living in London, became very interested in the watermen who took passengers up and down the river like modern cabbies. He donated the initial coat and badge that were the prize and organised the race every year until his death. Although there are far fewer watermen in the company today, winning the race is still a big deal. You can watch from the banks, best of all in Chelsea where the race reaches its triumphant end.
www.watermenshall.org

Bibi van der Zee

113

Summer

Camping without a tent

There can be few better ways of getting close to nature than sleeping in the midst of it, but even something as flimsy as a tent will form a barrier between your senses and the outside world. To get around this, simply set your spirit free and do away with the tent. After all, it's summer.

Caves

Never let us forget that the cave has been humanity's default des res for much longer than the Johnny-come-lately house. Indeed, there are some places around the world – Spain, Morocco and Turkey to name but three – where people still call a cave home.

So, if you fancy becoming a troglodyte for the night, your first task is to find your cave. Helpfully, large-scale Ordnance Survey maps mark the position of a great many of them with the word 'cave'. You'll find particularly rich concentrations in Assynt (in the far north-west of Scotland), Somerset's Mendip Hills and the Peak District, particularly around Castleton – Sir Arthur Conan Doyle suggested that the ground there was so hollow that that if hit with a hammer it would 'boom like a drum'.

Ideally, your cave should be dry, or at least have a large dry sleeping area within it, have an entrance that will shelter you from wind and is not in danger of being blocked by a nocturnal rock slide. A sea cave is not always a great choice, since it is often difficult to gauge whether it will flood at full tide. Unless you are absolutely certain that it is above the high spring tide line, you should look elsewhere for your night's kip: swimming for your life in pitch darkness at 2am is rarely a pleasurable experience.

ving

Around 6000 BC you'd have had stiff competition for this des-res gaff, but now it's all yours ...

Once you have chosen a suitable cave, make it as cosy as you can with the materials available to you. If you want to light a fire, do so outside and away from any rock faces. This will ensure that you do not smoke yourself out of your new home or cause the rock to heat, crack and fall on top of you.

You don't even need to find a fully fledged cave – take the Cromlech Boulders in Snowdonia's Llanberis Pass, for instance. By day this is a popular climbing location, but when night falls climbers habitually get out their sleeping bags and slide underneath the huge overhanging rocks seemingly created for this very purpose.

Trees

King Charles II famously hid in one and eco-warriors make their homes in them. However, unless you find a particularly accommodating tree with wide branches that spread as much horizontally as vertically, your best chance of a good night's sleep is to seek out the hollowed trunk of an English oak. Robin Hood was said to have his entire headquarters in such a tree, though if two of you can get in one and lie down, you're doing quite well. Head for the Midlands for the greatest concentration of English oaks, but be prepared to share your cosy hole with squirrels.

Pillboxes

In the dark days of the second world war when an invasion was thought inevitable, Britons feverishly mixed concrete to create defensive bunkers. Scores of these pillboxes can be found around the countryside today. Many are situated near the coast, but a surprising number were built inland at strategic points where it was felt they could hold up an advance. Some have been left open and make dry, if often musty, stopovers. Just make sure that your pillbox is not on private land and remember to treat it kindly – it is, after all, a little bit of British history.

Beaches

For the simplest non-tent camp out of all, simply pick a warm night on which you can be fairly sure that the rain will hold off and get your head down on a beach. A sandy strand makes for the softest bed, but even shingles can be moulded around your body to give some comfort, though if you take some sort of sleeping mat with you, you'll thank yourself in the morning. Just don't forget about the tide and don't dig a cave in a dune – they're notoriously unstable.

Tarps

If you don't quite feel prepared to go the whole hog and camp without any sort of cover, take along a tarpaulin (though only ever refer to it as a 'tarp' or no one will ever mistake you for Ray Mears). This should have eyelets at the corners and along the edges through which a strong cord can be passed. The joy of a tarp is that it can be strung up almost anywhere (ideally in an upside-down V shape), without enclosing you in a little bubble as a tent would. Just lie back, feel the soft breeze on your face and drift off.

Dixe Wills

Summer

Foraging by the sea

Most of us have picked blackberries or hazelnuts while strolling through the countryside. Far fewer ever think of grazing along the shoreline – yet there are plenty of seaside plants to tickle the taste buds. None of the following will make a satisfying meal in itself, but the pleasure derived from supplementing a dish with something truly wild is immeasurable. Just remember not to be greedy – harvest a little from each plant and leave some for other hungry travellers who may come after you.

Sea kale

A really hardy plant that loves shingle beaches, sea kale is easily recognisable by the fact that great bushes of it – often 2ft high and several feet across – will grow where no other plant even tries. If you think you've spotted one, check for wide waxy leaves resembling those of a cabbage. From June to August it can also be identified by its small, white, four-petalled flowers, which bloom in clusters.

It's not the leaves or flowers that you're after, but its white shoots and the lower end of its leaf stalks. The lower you can go, the better – indeed, if you can get at stalks that are buried, they will be less bitter. Cut a few stems from each plant with a good knife.

Although the shoots and stalks can be thrown into a salad, they are at their best when boiled for 10 minutes and added to cooked pasta with some chopped olives, lemon juice and butter (with some chopped walnuts too, if you have them to hand).

chilling

Sea buckthorn

You'll have no problem identifying this seaside shrub, which can be found all round the coast. It produces masses of narrow leaves interspersed with thousands of small, bright orange berries that often hang around from summer to the following spring.

As a bonus, the berries are very high in vitamin C. However, they are quite acidic, so rather than eat them raw, try pulping them and adding the juice to a sweet drink. Alternatively, they can be used to pep up a fruit pie or an apple crumble.

Pick them in winter and you'll have some competition from another forager – fieldfares descend on sea-buckthorn when there's not much else for them to eat. However, wait until spring to harvest and you'll find the berries will have fermented a little, making them taste vaguely alcoholic.

Rock samphire

Also known as St Peter's herb or 'poor man's asparagus', rock samphire is a common sight on cliffs on the west and south coasts of Britain. It's a member of the same family as cow parsley so, to identify it, look out for that distinctive umbrella of tiny flowers. In the case of samphire, these are yellow and blossom from July to October on a fleshy plant that grows no more than 30-40cm high and always in range of sea spray at high tide.

Pick the stems and leaves (avoiding any that are slimy). They can be added to salads but are tastier if boiled for 10 minutes and eaten like asparagus with a favourite condiment. Nothing if not adaptable, they can also be pickled or included in a chutney. If you wish to impress your friends as you clamber about the cliffs, you can casually mention that the plant gets name-checked in King Lear.

Laver

A common seaweed that grows all round the coast. The canny people of Pembrokeshire have a long tradition that survives to this day of picking laver, pureeing and bottling it, and selling it to tourists as bara lawr (laver bread). You, however, can keep your money in your pocket by looking for a seaweed easily identifiable by long (20cm), yet thin and shiny fronds. These lie on top of rocks turning from green, when young, to purple. If you find a seaweed that has little pockets of air like Bubble Wrap, you're looking at bladderwrack, which is inedible (by humans, at least).

Cut the laver fronds, taking care not to pull the plant away from the rock or you'll kill it. You can either use them in stews and soups, as the Chinese and Japanese do, or make it into laver bread. Doing this is simplicity itself: add some water to the laver in a pan and – stirring continuously, simmer until the laver has formed a pulp. Eat either straight away – rolled in oatmeal and fried – or pop it into a jar to consume within a few days.

Dixe Wills

121

Fooling a

Skiving off work

Oooh, is that a sore throat coming on? Or is it just mounting excitement at the thought of heading off to your favourite festival? They're easily confused – just ask anyone who has ever run out of holiday time but needed to get away for a weekend (in the case of the Big Chill, a rather long weekend: the gates open on Thursday morning, and it'll be at least Tuesday before you've recovered).

Skiving off work is one of the great summer sports, and workers across the UK make sure to get in plenty of practice each year. Research carried out by the CBI (Confederation of British Industry) found that employers believe 21m days are lost every year to employees bunking off, costing businesses as much as £1bn. And they're not happy about it. Tesco refuses to give sick pay for your first three days off due to illness, and Royal Mail rewards employees with a 100 per cent attendance record. Lie detector tests have been developed that can tell whether you really have a cold or are deliberately trying to sound hoarse. And smaller business have been reported to hire private detectives to track people who call in sick, especially around Christmas and weekends: 'There's no illness that I know of that occurs only on Mondays and Fridays,' sniffed a CBI representative.

In the face of all this, Britain's workforce are adopting the Blitz spirit and skiving off like troupers, despite the risks. Festival-goers are particularly creative in their excuses, going beyond the usual flu and food poisoning. "I fell off a wall," offers one punter. Another told his boss he had been beaten up, so needed time off to recover; the only flaw was that he had to then beat himself up, splitting his lip in a convincing manner, which rather put a damper on his weekend. Others take inspiration from the headlines: nasty attacks of the norovirus, Sars, bird flu, even foot & mouth were all popular excuses in their day – although you'd have to be pretty brave to go with the Ebola virus, which makes you bleed from every orifice. Depending on your boss, a murmured 'women's troubles' may suffice.

For those who take pride in their truthfulness, the Little Giant Encyclopedia of Outrageous Excuses points out that, in the journal of the American Medical

round

Association, 'beer drinker's finger' is listed as a genuine illness. Symptoms: 'swelling, bluish discoloration and wasting of finger caused by placing beer-can rings on finger'. At least chronic sufferers know that relief is, so to speak, at hand.

So you've got the excuses covered – but that may turn out to be the least of your problems. There are nearly 12,000 videos of Glastonbury on YouTube, and each year sees more footage going up on websites and TV. Do you really want the boss to see you hanging off the sound-stage scaffolding, swigging from a can with one hand and groping a stranger with the other? There's always the old 'it was my evil twin' line – but that won't explain why you've turned up on Monday morning (or Tuesday, or Wednesday), with a deep tan on just one side of your face after having dozed off in the sun, or nails ingrained with mud. In this situation, men may find that the women's beauty industry has much to offer. One strapping lad who spent the weekend in a field admits to having a quick mani/pedi and applying a lick of foundation before venturing back into the office. (He didn't have much trouble accessing his feminine side; after all, he'd spent most of the weekend in a grass skirt.)

Of course, if you're really determined to skive for as long as you like, have as good a time as you like, and be filmed as much as you like, there are two words no boss can satisfactorily answer: 'I quit.'

Top tips

- At festivals, disguise yourself in such a cunning costume that no one at work could possibly recognise you, should you happen to be photographed. Writing 'twat' on your forehead in lipstick usually works.

- Avoid posting updates on Facebook saying what an awesome time you're having. Your boss can see them too, you know.

- If you haven't called in sick in advance, get a mate to do it for you on the day. Screaming down the phone from just outside the dance tent is a bit of a giveaway.

- Consider yourself to be declaring solidarity with the rebels. In the early noughties, one anti-corporate group declared 6 April 'World Sick Day' - well worth celebrating.

- Don't go writing a book about it. One French woman had a hit with her bestseller, Hello Laziness, which really flew the flag for skiving; she advised opportunistic workers to convert to Islam or Judaism, so as to take advantage of more religious holidays. But she ended up facing a disciplinary tribunal.

- If you want to take your kids out of school, be honest with the head teacher, and respect his or her decision. The eye of Ofsted sees all.

- If by chance you catch sight of another colleague who is up to the same trick, we recommend giving the "skivers' salute"; head angled downwards, hand held up to forehead so as to shield the face, while legs move fast to remove you from the vicinity.

Carrie O'Grady

Festival People

I guess you would have to call me a festiphile. I've doggedly attended Glastonbury every year, even performed there, and have helped run the Clacton festival for several years. So when my fiance Charlie looked up from his whittling one summer's day and said, 'Let's have a festival wedding,' I enthusiastically agreed.

When we had talked about our wedding before that, we'd fretted that there's nothing to do at such events except drink and stare at the bride and groom, drink some more and watch cousins scuffle in the car park. Being terminally shy, we were delighted to hit upon a way of distracting our guests' attention away from us. And so the concept of the 'nuptival' was born.

Having picked a date in October, we invited a hundred people to my parents' house and wished for sunshine.

Hannah Borno
festival bride

As part of our great policy of distraction, we decreed that all guests should wear capes and quasi-historical dress based on the theme 'autumns past'. We booked a brilliant acid-folk band called Circulus (who serendipitously also all wore capes).

Kind friends helped us dress the sheds, creating a pub with a shove-ha'penny board and kegs of real ale, a cider barn with straw bale benches and baskets of local apples, and a psychedelic disco decorated with giant nude mannequins and seashells. We wreathed trees in fairy lights and created a Victorian tearoom. We dug a fire pit in a small camping field behind the house. It was a miniature fantasy world of magic and misdirection.

On the day, we did the official register office bit in the morning then donned our fancier garb for our spiritual ceremony in the afternoon. We each burned a lock of our hair and mingled the ashes to plant under a conker sapling. Was it a mistake to force the bewildered congregation to sing Climb Ev'ry Mountain from The Sound of Music to dulcimers? Opinion remains divided.

Then it was champagne, sound therapy and hula hooping with Sharna Rose, who runs workshops at Glastonbury. A dozen hoopers swivelled and wiggled under Sharna's expert eye. I glanced over at my husband of two hours. He was lying down within a circle of chanting guests cleansing his chakras. Other guests ate scones and cake at the all-day tea party, or hung out in the pub or cider barn. Some drifted to the chill-out room for an Indian head massage or aromatherapy, while others met their ancestors in a guided group meditation or had their feet squeezed and patted by a foot therapist. The chiropody option proved popular with the older guests.

Our first dance was in a fairy-lit courtyard to the evocative strains of Circulus, who played giddying psychedelic folk for far longer than we had paid them to. We gathered round the bonfire for fire-eating, juggling and Sharna's stunning fire hula-hoop performance, followed by a firework display, minstrel performances and drunken fire leaping. Guests then meandered about, swigging from pewter tankards, visiting the disco or singing by the fire pit till dawn.

Best of all, it didn't rain. Our huge white nuptial tent never made it up, so Charlie and I spent our wedding night crashed out fully clothed with other tentless nuptival-goers on a straw-strewn floor under the stable rafters.

The downside? Instead of contemplating our solemn lifelong commitment, we spent much of the day running around looking for cash to pay the performers. My sister, who worked tirelessly, missed the band and fireworks while others who had offered to help were distracted by champagne. But almost everyone had been transported into another world for a tiny while – and nobody had been bored. The usual wedding stresses miraculously evaporated. Small details like booking a photographer, finding something to wear to the register office or buying shoes for the big day had completely escaped my notice. And I hadn't given hair or makeup a single thought – I was too busy booking fire-eaters.

Dish of the

Poulet basquaise

From Big Chill regulars La Grande Bouffe

Ingredients:

6 fleshy chicken legs

500ml dry white wine

About 30 green olives (not compulsory but if your guests like them they are very tasty)

750ml tomato juice

5 big juicy fresh tomatoes

2 tbsp olive oil

1 tbsp cornflour

3 or 4 garlic cloves

3 or 4 branches thyme or 1 tbsp Provençal herbs

2 big bay leaves

Salt and pepper, and celery salt if you can find it

La Grande Bouffe
✳ **THE BIG NOSH** ✳

Method:

First of all, put some great music on. Pour yourself a glass of your favourite wine. Start dancing along. Once you are well in the groove, pour the olive oil into a big heavy-based pot and, at medium heat, roast the chicken legs on both sides until golden. Season with salt (and celery salt), pepper and garlic (this dish requires quite a lot of salt because of the tomatoes). As your chicken legs are getting deliciously golden, slice your fresh tomatoes and put them aside.

Sip a bit more of your wine, do a twirl and check on your chicken. When the colour is right, in go the tomatoes. Give them a stir, then pour the tomato juice and dry white wine into your saucepan. Add the herbs and olives.

After five minutes, taste the gravy for seasoning, season to your taste, reduce heat to the minimum, put on a lid and let simmer for 30 minutes. Add some cornflour to thicken the gravy if needed and let simmer for a further 15 minutes. Serve on a bed of rice or potatoes with a big green salad.

Drink of th

SoCo smash

From the Big Chill bartenders

Shake all the ingredients together with cubed ice and **strain** into a glass with more ice.

SOUTHERN COMFORT

40ml Southern Comfort
15ml lime juice
15ml passion fruit syrup
15ml passion fruit puree
60ml cranberry juice
One orange twist

Game of

Worm charming

All you need is a piece of grass and a bit of know-how to get everyone involved in this cheery pastime. It's a delightful, albeit unconventional, way to pass an afternoon in the park or on a campsite.

According to the official rules (yes, there is an official set of rules), each competitor has a three-by-three square metre plot of land and 30 minutes to entice as many earthworms out of the ground as possible. Various techniques have been tried and tested over the years, but the most successful one, 'twanging', involves sticking a four-pronged garden fork about 15cm into the ground and wiggling it about.

As garden forks aren't always readily available, you might have to be a little more inventive with your approach. Anything that makes the ground vibrate is good – worms typically squirm to the surface because they think the movements are coming from their natural predator, the mole – and common techniques include playing music to the ground and tap-dancing on it. Some charmers swear by more unconventional methods, though, such as meditation, or pouring a mixture of gravy, beer and sugar into the ground. Why not be imaginative and see what new techniques you can come up with?

Whatever you do, always be considerate to our little wriggly friends: don't harm them in any way (a method using knitting needles once went very wrong at an event in Cheshire), put them in a damp area during the competition and release them once they have been counted.

So how many worms should you expect? It's entirely dependent on the weather and type of soil, but aim high. The world record was set 29 years ago by teenager Tom Shufflebotham: he charmed 511.

www.wormcharming.com

Perri Lewis

July festival directory

MUSIC

THE BIG ONES

Isle of Wight Festival
When: Mid July
Where: Seaclose Park, Newport, Isle of Wight
Cost: Weekend including camping is £140
Website: www.isleofwightfestival.com
Famous for hosting the last major performance by Jimi Hendrix and revived in 2003 into a much more run-of-the-mill affair, it still attracts rock royalty like David Bowie, Neil Diamond and the Stones.

Latitude
When: Mid July
Where: Southwold, Suffolk
Cost: £130 weekend, £55 day, children free
Website: www.latitudefestival.co.uk
Run by the same promoters who do Glastonbury, Reading and Leeds – which gives you a flavour of things – there's a surprisingly generous dollop of literature, theatre and art alongside the usual musical suspects.

Oxegen
When: Early/Mid July
Where: Punchestown Racecourse, Naas, Co Kildare
Cost: 224 euros for a weekend pass.
Website: www.oxegen.ie
The same weekend and (mostly) the same line up as T in the Park, this is Ireland so the craic will be legendary even if you do spend most of the weekend dashing between stages, Guinness in hand.

T in the Park
When: Early/Mid July
Where: Balado, Kinross-shire
Cost: Weekend including camping is £160.
Website: www.tinthepark.com
A reliable serving of massive global names and the year's biggest acts – the 2009 line-up includes a reformed Blur, Yeah Yeah Yeahs and Elbow. People camp outside record stores to get tickets for this one.

Wireless
When: Early July
Where: Hyde Park, London
Cost: £40 day ticket. £139 Club Experience Package. £179 VIP Experience Package.
Website: www.wirelessfestival.co.uk
Smack in the heart of London and offering headliners like Jay-Z, Fatboy Slim and the White Stripes...the list goes on. Big crowds, big names and sponsored up to the eyeballs but plenty to enjoy nonetheless.

Womad
When: Late July
Where: Charlton Park, Malmmesbury, Wilts
Cost: £122.34 weekend ticket, £24.46 Thursday camping ticket, children free.
Website: www.womad.org
Miriam thumb piano, Uzbekistani opera, Celtic 'acid croft' beats – there's something for everyone at the festival that put world music centre stage in the early eighties and has kept it there since.

ROCK/INDIE

2000 Trees
When: Early July
Where: Upcote Farm, Withington, Cheltenham
Cost: £39 adult, £20 10-15 years, under 10s free
Website: www.twothousandtreesfestival.co.uk
The combo of cheap, ethical, green and generally ace has proved so popular the original cap on tickets has been stretched by an extra 500 (so, 2500 Trees, surely?). Still good and small compared to the corporate mega festivals it was set up to counter.

Blissfields
When: Early July
Where: The Matterly Bowl, Winchester
Cost: £60 adult, £40 youth, free for children under eight
Website: www.blissfields.co.uk
Named after founders Paul and Mel Bliss – a fortuitous surname to be sure – this is an award-winning small festival. You are politely requested to leave bad attitudes and musical small-mindedness at home.

BOMFest
When: Mid July
Where: Locke Park, Barnsley
Cost: around £5 in advance
Website: www.bomfest.com
You might not think there's enough new music in Barnsley to warrant a whole festival. Six successful BOMfests proves you wrong, so ner. Showcasing local unsigned talent playing original music.

Camp Bestival
When: Late July
Where: Lulworth Castle, Dorset.
Cost: adult weekend ticket £120, child age 12-16 £60, under 12s free
Website: www.campbestival.co.uk
Reviving the spirit of the 1950s British holiday camp but without the postwar deprivation presumably. Bluecoats and ironic touches plus top acts, boutique camping, a pamper lounge and a River Cottage café. Hi de hi.

Cockermouth Rock Festival (Cock Rock)
When: Mid July
Where: Outskirts of Cockermouth, Cumbria
Cost: around £25 for w/e pass. £15 a day. Concessions available.
Website: www.cockermouthrockfestival.com
Organisers clearly don't take themselves too seriously – did you notice the name of this festival – but they're serious about their mission to support local musicians and local charities. Rock on.

Guilfest
When: Early July
Where: Guildford, Surrey
Cost: £100 adult, £40 child
Website: www.guilfest.co.uk
Once a folk event, now an established Glasto style mix of genres, if the showers aren't to your liking, take a dip in the lido next door. Ooh, and there's a 140 foot bar which either makes it very hard or very easy to get served.

Heavenly Planet
When: Early/Mid July
Where: Richfield Avenue, Rivermead, Reading, Berkshire
Cost: around £70 for a weekend ticket
Website: www.heavenlyplanetfestival.co.uk
Curmudgeons beware, this brand new festival is about celebrating optimism through the medium of music, dance and the spoken word. So positively no griping if it rains and your tent leaks.

Hop Farm Festival
When: Early July
Where: Hop Farm, Paddock Wood, Kent
Cost: Tickets £54
Website: www.hopfarmfestival.com
An ex-Reading festival boss has gone back to basics. No VIP area, no branding and no

Party Belgian-style at the raucous
Dour Festival.

sponsorship, just a distinctly starry line up with the likes of Rufus Wainwright, Primal Scream and Neil Young.

Indietracks
When: Late July
Where: Midland Railway, Butterly, Derbyshire
Cost: £45 weekend, £25 day
Website: www.indietracks.co.uk
While you might not normally welcome live music on the train here it's all part of the strangely successful pairing of steam trains and indie festival. For a happy few that must be a match made in heaven.

Lakeside Magic
When: Early-Mid June
Where: Kingston Maurward, Dorchester, Dorset
Cost: around £20 in advance to £24 on gate. Extra charge for seats.
Website: www.lakesidemagic.biz
Tribute bands – Abba 2 Bjorn Belief, anyone? – in the grounds of a stately home. Park up your caravan and take your seats on the terrace for dinner and a prime view. The presence of hospitality marquees tells its own tale.

Lounge on the Farm
When: Mid July
Where: Merton Farm, Canterbury, Kent
Cost: £85 adult weekend, £45 child and £180 family weekend
Website: www.loungeonthefarm.co.uk
There's a healthy (and proper working farm) whiff of manure about this new kid on the block. A world away from other identikit festivals, food is locally sourced and the cider flows freely all weekend.

Lovebox Weekender
When: Mid July
Where: Victoria Park, East London
Cost: £38.50 one day, £65 both days.
Website: www.lovebox.net
A perfectly formed little beauty with a carnival atmosphere, food from Borough Market and everyone seems to be in a good mood. Expect the likes of the Go! Team and Goldfrapp to join festival founders Groove Armada on the bill.

Monmouth Festival
When: Late July/Early August
Where: Blestium St. Carpark, Monmouth, South Wales
Cost: FREE
Website: www.monmouthfestival.co.uk
Punk, reggae, rock, folk, swing, R&B, rap, male voice choirs… and that's just the music. You also get a street carnival, a road race and a dog show. And it's all free.

Nozstock Festival
When: End July/Early August
Where: Bromyard, Herefordshire
Cost: around £40
Website: www.nozstockfestival.co.uk
Comedy, theatricals, bands and other standard festival fare aside, of particular note here are the former bullpen and cowshed transformed into cocoons of dance where the walls shake to heart-rattling loud basslines into the wee hours.

Secret Garden Party
When: Late July
Where: Abbots Rippon, Huntingdon
Cost: £125 adults, £100 over 14, children free
Website: www.secretgardenparty.com
Like some kind of crazy love child spawned by Burning Man and a decadent house party, this is a high concept festival where 'gardeners' are positively encouraged to join in. Mind bending costumes, floating stages and bizarre stuff round every corner.

Summer Series
When: Early/Mid July
Where: Somerset House, London
Cost: £25 plus booking fee for each gig.
Website: www.somersethouse.org.uk
No tent pitching, no slipping about in mud, no warm beer. What kind of festival is this? It's not, it's top acts – Duffy, The Zutons etc – playing a series of outdoor gigs throughout July in one of London's smartest venues.

SuperSonic

When: Mid July
Where: Custard Factory, Birmingham
Cost: £65 weekend, £15 Friday, £35 Saturday, £30 Sunday,
Website: www.myspace.com/supersonic
In the place where metal, experimental music and cake meet (yes, there is such a place) you'll find Supersonic, an avant garde noise fest that takes up a whole block of Birmingham's industrial centre. Very, very (very) loud.

Truck

When: Mid July
Where: Hill Farm, Steventon
Cost: £60 for the weekend
Website: www.thisistruck.com
The original boutique festival and still resolutely anti-commercial. Ice cream is sold by the local vicar, profits go to charity and it attracts around 5,000 converts through the barn door every year.

The Wickerman Festival

When: Late July
Where: East Kirkcarswell near Dundrennan South West Scotland
Cost: £80 w/e includes camping
Website: www.thewickermanfestival.co.uk
There is 25-foot burning effigy, yes, and some scenes from the cult horror movie were filmed in the area but this counter-culture festival is entirely family-friendly with oldies and youngsters partying hard side by side.

FOLK

Cambridge Folk Festival

When: Late July/Early August
Where: Cherry Hinton Hall, Cambridge, Cambridgeshire
Cost: around £100 for full weekend
Website: www.cambridgefolkfestival.co.uk
Folk? That barely begins to describe what's on offer here. Expect a mouthwatering mix of names like KD Lang, Joan Baez, Emmylou Harris, Judy Collins and Paul Simon. Going since the 60s and now an institution.

Celtic Blue Rock Festival

When: Friday Late July/Early August
Where: Llanfyrnach fields, Pembrokeshire
Cost: Early bird ticket at £30 for the weekend.
Website: www.celticbluerock.org.uk
This is a community festival with real bite, taking on the Welsh Assembly, teaching the young folk how to run music events and promoting the local credit union as a way to pay for your ticket. Power to the (folk) people.

Ely Folk Festival

When: Early/Mid July
Where: Ely Outdoor Centre, Ely, Cambridgeshire
Cost: around £55/£40 (concs); kids 10-16 yrs - £18 Camping £8 / £4 (kids) each
Website: www.elyfolk.co.uk
We're guessing there's no mosh pit at a festival that lets you bring your folding chairs into the marquees – as long as you don't obscure anyone else's view, of course. Small town festival with an up close and personal vibe.

Glastonwick

When: Early July
Where: Coombes Farm, Coombes, West Sussex
Cost: around £7 a day
Website: www.myspace.com/glastonwick; www.cask-ale.co.uk/beerfestival
Bands and poets are handpicked by charismatic host/compere Attila the Stockbroker but we humbly suggest that it's the 65 cask conditioned ales that form the main event. No crappy festival beer here, no siree.

Gloucester Rhythm and Blues Festival

When: Late/Early August
Where: Gloucester
Cost: around £12.50 for ticketed events; all other Main Stage and pub events are free.
Website: www.gloucesterblues.co.uk
Good old-fashioned, down-dirty homemade blues festival mixing up international and local acts. The cheerful crowd includes a lot of kids and a good few grannies too.

Hebridean Celtic Festival

When: Mid July
Where: Outer Hebrides, Scotland
Cost: expect season ticket around £60
Website: www.hebceltfest.com
Is it us or does folk music sound better in a rugged Celtic setting where most of the locals speak Gaelic? Stornoway largely shuts down on a Sunday so you'll have no choice but to slow down and chill out.

Kelvedon Festival

When: Mid July
Where: Kelvedon , Essex
Cost: Free
Website: www.kelvedonfreemusicfestival.co.uk
One stage (okay, a truck), acts mostly from Essex, a beer tent that funds everything and – since getting a generator in 2001 – powered up! Organised by local people for the local community.

Larmer Tree Festival

When: Mid July
Where: Larmer Tree Gardens, nr Tollard Royal, on the Wilts/Dorset border
Cost: 3 day adult £115, youth £95, child £75, under 5s are free
Website: www.larmertreefestival.co.uk
Who fancies a top-notch jazz/blues/folk festival in a Victorian pleasure garden? This has solid gold family friendly credentials, an extremely loyal following and the occasional peacock ambling across the stage.

Lomond Folk Festival

When: Late July
Where: Balloch, 20 miles north of Glasgow
Cost: around £27 for weekend, many free events.
Website: www.lomondfolkfestival.com
Nothing raises the spirits quicker than a wee dram, some fiery fiddle playing and a death-defying whirl around the floor of a ceilidh. If you're on the banks of bonny Loch Lomond, all the better.

Music for Africa

When: Early July
Where: Montacute, Nr Yeovil, Somerset
Cost: Adults £18 per night, Children £9, family £42.
Website: www.musicforafrica.org.uk

The colourful harbour of Stornoway on the Isle of Lewis.

Give something back through the medium of dancing yourself stupid all weekend. The money you spend enjoying yourself helps buy instruments for African school children and pays for music teachers.

National Forest Folk Festival
When: Early July
Where: Conkers, near Ashby-de-la-Zouch, Leicestershire
Cost: £54 weekend
Website: www.affc.demon.co.uk
From the town that distributes Jacobs Cream Crackers comes a folk festival held in a Conker Visitor Centre. Not very rock and roll, maybe, but wonderfully folky and extremely welcoming.

Scarborough Seafest
When: Mid July
Where: the harbour area, Scarborough, North Yorkshire
Cost: Free
Website: www.seafest.org.uk
What do you get when you cross fish and folk music? Seafood cookery demos, maritime arts, a smattering of Captain Birdseye beards and a lot of sea shanties.

Sidmouth Folk Week
When: Late July/Early August
Where: Sidmouth, Devon
Cost: Adult full week £160, youth £70, child £35, under 7 free.
Website: www.sidmouthfolkweek.co.uk
Crab sarnies, cream teas, social dances and stripy deckchairs, this is folk music beside the seaside and all the breezier for it. Award winning acts and audiences from all over the world.

Singing Sticks Didgeridoo Festival
When: Early/Mid July
Where: Overstone Scout Camp, Overstone, Northants
Cost: early bird offer £25 then £30, children (10 to 15) £3 then £5
Website: www.singingsticks.co.uk
If you go down to the woods today…

you'll stumble across hoards of laid back didgeridoo enthusiasts and outdoorsy ravers, rubbing shoulders and celebrating circular breathing.

Spratton Folk Festival
When: Early/Mid July
Where: Spratton, Northamptonshire
Cost: expect around £35
Website: www.sprattonfestival.com
What village festival would be complete without emergency service displays, a pig roast and a mobile chippy? Expect a traditional mix of folk music, dance troupes and market stalls.

Stonehaven Folk Festival
When: Early Mid July
Where: Stonehaven, North East Scotland
Cost: expect around £65 for 4 day pass
Website: www.stonehavenfolkfestival.co.uk
Okay, so they can't guarantee the best weather or the most refined food (ever wondered where the deep fried Mars bar was dreamt up?) but you will get folk circuit legends and a warm welcome.

Warwick Folk festival
When: Late July
Where: Warwick school grounds, Warwick
Cost: around £60 early bird
Website: www.warwickfolkfestival.co.uk
Big names like Kate Rusby and Jim Moray plus back room sessions, singarounds, meet the artists, ceilidhs, workshops etc. Everything you'd expect from a festival that's beaten off the competition for thirty odd years.

WOMAD Festival
When: Late July
Where: Charlton Park, Malmesbury, Wiltshire
Cost: £125 camping weekend ticket, £50 day
Website: www.womad.org
World music festivals can come across a bit worthy and dull but Womad has spun-off into a global phenomenon for a reason. Expect some incredible sounds, tons of energy and great food.

Mixing a perfect summer vibe at Croatia's Garden Festival.

DANCE/ELECTRONICA

Glade
When: Mid/Late July
Where: Secret Berkshire location. Details with ticket
Cost: Tickets £125
Website: www.gladefestival.com
Underground electronic music played organ-shakingly loud now that they've changed venues and can crank it up longer and later, this is anti-corporate raving at its best from the people behind the original renegade dance area at Glastonbury.

Global Gathering
When: Late July 2009
Where: Long Marston Airfield, nr. Stratford on Avon, Warwickshire
Cost: adult weekend £126.50.
Website: www.globalgathering.co.uk
If 55,000 up-for-it festival goers sweating along to the likes of Orbital and the Prodigy sounds a bit much you can always buy VIP tickets for the Golden Circle and rub glow sticks with an altogether better class of person.

CLASSICAL/JAZZ

Boogie Woogie Festival
When: Early July
Where: Sturminster Newton and Fiddleford, Dorset
Cost: expect an all event ticket to be around £65 per person
Website: www.ukboogiewoogiefestival. co.uk
Get up out of your seat and swing your partner over your head, this is three days of infectious, foot tapping boogie woogie thrills. You can even tinkle the ivories along with the pros at an open piano session.

Budleigh Festival – Music and the Arts
When: Late July
Where: Budleigh Salterton, East Devon
Cost: from around £3 - £16 adults. Half price for kids. Family tickets available
Website: www.budleigh-festival.org.uk
For a small Devon town, Budleigh Salterton has serious festival credentials. Visitors can expect eight days of quality classical, early and contemporary music plus literature, drama and lunchtime talks.

Cheltenham Music Festival

When: Early/Mid July
Where: Venues throughout Cheltenham, Gloucestershire
Cost: Events priced individually
Website: www.cheltenhamfestivals.com
Gold standard festival of orchestral, chamber, choral and solo music that's been going since 1945 and has hosted well over 250 world premiers in its time.

Manchester International Festival – Music Series

When: Early July
Where: venues around Manchester
Cost: various prices dependent on event
Website: www.mif.co.uk
Calling this classical isn't really the full story. Think operas by the likes of Damon Albarn and Rufus Wainwright, new theatre starring Johnny Vegas, food by Heston Blumenthal and music from Gossip, amongst others. Seriously good stuff.

Manchester Jazz Festival

When: Mid July
Where: Venues throughout Manchester including St Ann's Square, City Inn Hotel and Matt & Phred's jazz club.
Cost: Events priced individually
Website: www.manchesterjazz.com
Cutting edge contemporary jazz isn't everyone's cup of tea but if it's yours, then this is absolutely the festival for you. New works, international artists and a real melting pot of styles and influences. Nice!

Swanage Jazz Festival

When: Mid July
Where: Various venues around town
Cost: Events priced individually
Website: www.swanagejazz.org.uk
Oh we do like to bebop beside the seaside – and swing and jive etc. Venues include a traditional bandstand and a boat cruise. Gentle, enjoyable fun with a loyal jazz following.

Tired of mud and noise? Retreat to the genteel charms of Winchester.

INTERNATIONAL

Dour Festival
When: Mid July
Where: Dour, Belgium
Cost: 85 euros, £45 per day
Website: www.dourfestival.be
The name refers to the location rather than the vibe, in case you were wondering. Thousands of alternative music lovers can attest to the fact that this is actually a big phat party from start to finish.

Exit Festival
When: Early July
Where: Petrovaradin Fortress, Novi Sad, Serbia
Cost: around £75 for the four days, camping £14 extra
Website: www.exitfest.org
It's the political edge running through Exit (the first event was a rebellion against the Milosevic regime) that raises it above your average hedonistic festival. Expect a very special atmosphere and big acts in their element.

Festival Internacional de Benicassim
When: Mid July
Where: Benicassim, nr Valencia, Spain
Cost: 155 euros per ticket
Website: www.fiberfib.com
Could it be the guaranteed Spanish sunshine that attracts the big names and big crowds to FIB? Whatever, alongside more obvious acts there are usually a few rarer treats like Antony and the Johnsons and the Pixies.

Fuji Rock Festival
When: Late July
Where: Naeba Ski Resort, Japan
Cost: £200 festival pass, camping extra
Website: www.smash-uk.com/frf09/
Forget greasy chips, smelly portaloos and the same old festival vibe. Try it the Japanese way – big acts in a mountain location with hot spring baths, the cleanest facilities in the world (apparently) and traditional Japanese food.

The Garden Festival
When: Early July and throughout the summer
Where: Petrcane, Near Zadar, Croatia
Cost: £70 for the weekend
Website: www.thegardenfestival.eu
World class DJs, a beachfront complex, daily boat parties and numbers capped at 2,000 equal extreme fun in the sun. So much so, organisers have extended things into a whole summer season.

Rock Werchter
When: Early July
Where: Leuven, Nr Brussels, Belgium
Cost: 165 euro weekender
Website: www.rockwerchter.be
Belgium's biggest festival shapes up much like all the other mega festivals – multiple stages, massive crowds and the likes of Radiohead, Jay-Z, Oasis and Coldplay on the programme.

Roskilde
When: Early July
Where: Roskilde, Denmark
Cost: £115 weekender
Website: www.roskilde-festival.dk
The days when Dr Hook performed here butt naked are long gone (sadly). This is now one of Europe's big four along with Sziget, Rock Werchter and Glasto, who are all pretty similar in terms of line up and vibe too.

ARTS

The Big Green Gathering
When: Late July
Where: Somerset
Cost: adults £125, children under 12 free and 12-17 £50
Website: www.big-green-gathering.com
Blowing most festival's green credentials out of the water – pedal-powered stage, lessons in permaculture, heated debate – this one was spawned by the Green Fields at Glastonbury so there's also a whole lot of healing going on.

Buxton Festival

When: Early-mid July
Where: Venues in Buxton, Derbyshire
Cost: Events are individually priced
Website: www.buxtonfestival.co.uk
Unmissable for the opera buff – Buxton specialises in rarely performed opera – but also friendly and accessible enough to please the complete novice. Plenty of top quality music and literature too.

Henley Festival

When: Early/Mid July
Where: Throughout Henley on Thames, Oxfordshire
Cost: Events individually priced
Website: www.henley-festival.co.uk
Hot on the heels of Regatta week welcome to the glamour end of the festival circuit. This is a posh frock affair with dinner parties on the river, jazz, opera, street theatre, floating stages and fireworks.

Liverpool Arabic Arts Festival

When: Mid/Late July
Where: Venues throughout Liverpool city centre
Cost: Events individually priced
Website: www.arabicartsfestival.co.uk
A fixture on the arts scene long before there was a sniff of culture capital in the air, this is an exotic mix of BAFTA winning films, traditional storytelling, performing arts and delish food from one of the UK's oldest ethnic communities.

Winchester Festival

When: Early/Mid July
Where: Venues throughout Winchester, including the cathedral
Cost: Events individually priced
Website: www.winchesterfestival.co.uk
Perambulate like a Jane Austen heroine round this genteel festival and you may just bump into president and all round national treasure, Dame Judi. If not, you'll still get a reliably good mix of visual arts, theatre, music and refined walks.

LITERATURE/WRITTEN WORD

BBC Proms Literary Festival

When: Throughout July to September
Where: Royal Albert Hall (also broadcast on BBC Radio 3)
Cost: Many events are free
Website: www.bbc.co.uk/proms
For those Prommers who see it as a badge of honour to go to every concert, there's now a series of literary talks hooked around the themes of the season. A whole new level of addiction beckons for some.

Dartington Hall Festival – Ways With Words

When: Early/Mid July
Where: Dartington Hall, Totnes, South Devon
Cost: £8 for individual events, day tickets from £30, subject to change.
Website: www.ways-with-words.co.uk
Is there anything more thrilling to the avid reader than the chance to rub shoulders with their favourite authors? Here you get ten whole days with writers like Kate Mosse, Tony Benn and Penelope Lively. Bookish bliss.

Festival at the Edge

When: Month of July
Where: Stokes Barn, Much Wenlock, Shropshire
Cost: Events individually priced
Website: www.festivalattheedge.org
Are you sitting comfortably? Kick back and rediscover the simple pleasure of having someone read you a story. Tall tales, music and workshops in the ridiculously picturesque village of Much Wenlock.

Harrogate Crime Writing Festival

When: Late July
Where: The Crown Hotel, Harrogate
Cost: Events individually priced
Website: www.harrogate-festival.org.uk
Forensically pick over every aspect of the genre alongside authors like Stella Duffy, Val McDermid and Christopher Brookmyre. There's even a quiz to sort the criminally obsessed from the mildly interested.

Hucknall International Byron Festival

When: End June/Early July
Where: Ashfield, Hucknall and surrounding places associated with Lord Byron
Cost: Many events are free
Website: www.ashfield-dc.gov.uk/ccm/navigation/leisure-and-culture/arts-and-entertainment/byron-festival/

A collection of loosely Byron-themed events, there are heritage walks and exhibitions (so far, so sensible) but also, somewhat bizarrely, a tie-in with a sports festival and a nothing-at-all-to-do-with-Byron X-factor style talent show.

Port Eliot Literature Festival

When: Late July
Where: Port Eliot Estate, St Germans, Cornwall
Cost: Adult weekend ticket £90, Child weekend ticket £35, Family weekend ticket £225
Website: www.porteliotlitfest.com

Not your average lit fest, this has the craic of a music festival with the vibe of a garden party. Previous highlights include Louis de Bernieres playing his mandolin and a John Betjeman poetry slam.

FILM

RAI International Festival of Ethnographic Film

When: Early July
Where: Venues at Leeds universities, plus Bradford Media Museum
Cost: currently unknown
Website: www.raifilmfest.org.uk

An incredibly diverse programme of films, workshops and discussion organised by the Royal Anthropological Institute and hosted by a different UK university every two years.

Swale Film Festival

When: Early July
Where: Avenue Theatre, Sittingbourne and Screen on Sheppey, Sheerness, Kent
Cost: Events individually priced
Website: www.swalefilmfestival.org.uk

With a mission to share the magic of film with the people of Swale, there are screenings, workshops and awards to encourage budding filmmakers to get creative.

OUTDOORS

Dance Al Fresco

When: one Saturday in July and one in August
Where: The Broadwalk, Avenue Gardens, Regent's Park, London
Cost: £10 per person for each day
Website: www.dancealfresco.org

Lock yourself in a passionate embrace with a complete stranger and if there's a summer deluge, just squeeze up and dance under your umbrella. Buenos Aires comes to Regents Park with a gloriously surreal celebration of exotic dance.

Waterman's Race

When: July (dates vary according to tide)
Where: River Thames – London Bridge to Chelsea
Cost: Free to spectate
Website: www.watermenshall.org

Every year since 1715 six Thames watermen have raced single sculls from London Bridge to Chelsea in the Doggett's Coat and Badge Race. An almost unknown piece of London history that you can watch from the riverbank.

ALTERNATIVE ENTERTAINMENT

Ashburton Bread Weighing and Ale Tasting Ceremony

When: third Saturday in July
Where: Ashburton town centre, Devon
Cost: Free
Website: www.ashburton.org

Not an obvious choice for a festival. Ale tasting, fair enough, but is there much fun

Slave to the rhythm? Then grab a partner at Dance Al Fresco.

to be had weighing bread? Luckily there's a procession and a medieval fair too, to liven things up.

Cumbria Steam Gathering
When: LateJuly
Where: Cark Airfield, Flookburgh, Cumbria
Cost: See website
Website: www.steamgathering.org.uk
Drive a tractor, pore over vintage farm vehicles, carve sculptures with chainsaws. Damn it, there are even wrestling bouts. Boys and their toys, and all with the heady smell of steam engines in the air.

Furness Tradition Festival
When: Mid July
Where: Ulverston, Cumbria
Cost: £30 per adult weekend ticket, £83.20 per family
Website: www.furnesstradition.org.uk
This self-proclaimed festival town doesn't need much excuse to put on a party. Most of them seem to involve ale and a spot of dancing. This one is no exception – dance, storytelling, music, beer drinking etc.

Tewkesbury Medieval Festival
When: Early July
Where: Fields off Lincoln Green Lane, Tewkesbury
Cost: Free entry
Website: www.tewkesburymedievalfestival.org
This is 'the' re-enactment event on the circuit (yes, there's a circuit) with warts and all beheadings, battles and other authentically gruesome goings on. The person responsible for lost property must have some stories.

FOOD & DRINK

Lavender Festival
When: Early July
Where: The Hop Farm, Shoreham, Sevenoaks, Kent TN14 7UB
Cost: Entry is free, tours are £4 for adults, free for under 14s
Website: www.hopshop.co.uk/festival

Breathe in and relax. Just twenty miles from central London you can tour an idyllic lavender farm, eat cakes with the WI, sample lavender flavoured foods and get an aromatherapy massage in amongst the lavender rows. Bliss.

Pontefract Liquorice Festival
When: Mid July
Where: Pontefract town centre, venues
Cost: Most events are free
Website: www.pontefractliquorice.co.uk
Savour the sweet smell that hangs over the town and sample all manner of Wonka-esque liquorice goodies. Unless you fall into the camp that can't abide the stuff in which case avoid Pontefract in July like the plague.

Whitstable Oyster Fair
When: Mid/Late July
Where: Whitstable Harbour area, Kent
Cost: Free
Website: www.whitstableoysterfestival.co.uk
Who knew oysters had a patron saint? Well they do and around his feast day the people of Whitstable spend nine whole days worshipping the slippery little suckers with fish slapping, parades, dancing and other salty shenanigans.

Emma McGowan

augu

'A smile four days wide'
– E Harvey

illustration Andy J Miller

tHE BiGCHiLL festival

Herefordshire

www.bigchill.net

Is there a line-up at any festival anywhere quite as eclectic, as surprising, or as inviting, as the line-up at The Big Chill? In just a few hours you can journey through disco fever, wacked-out comedy, and thumpin' bumpin house, to an elegant guitar set in the last rays of the sun, with a cracked-baritone pop star to send you to sleep.

It's all very very right for the festival that never intended to get so big. Starting life as a series of parties in Islington's Union Chapel in 1994, The Big Chill lifted themselves up and became a party for 700 people the following year in the Black Mountains in Wales. In 1998 it moved to the Larmer Tree Gardens in Wiltshire and then eventually ended up in its idyllic current home in the grounds of Eastnor Castle, with the glorious Malvern Hills in the distance.

Nowadays, some 30,000 festival goers descend upon the site for a three day party every year, and yet the festival has somehow retained the intimate feel that leaves long-time fans reminiscing on the Big Chill Forum about 'the time we arrived and there was just one marquee and one café tent. We asked a steward if that was it and he replied "Oh no, there's another field through there with a stream and trees in it".' The festival organisers, you feel, spend their year collecting funky things for their gig as obsessively as any trainspotter. Hence the busker's stage for anyone who wants to get up and have a go, or the chocolate parlour, or the whiskey bar in a treehouse with a capacity of just fifteen. There is passionate

The Big Chill's big tree lit at night; (left) Blue Man Group giving it some.

The Big Chill festival in full swing. Above: The Mighty Boosh cleverly disguised as nanas. Left: space hopper racing!

attention to your enjoyment (to the extent that Big Chill wins the festival toilet award year after year), which means that yes the music is good, but everything else is good too.

Part of the unique charm of this event comes from the (often surprising) mixture of musical styles on offer, which sees headliners such as Leonard Cohen, Orbital and Isaac Hayes on the same bill as smaller, but no less accomplished acts like The Ukelelé Orchestra of Great Britain, world music fusion-pioneers Tiniwaren, or beat-boxer extraordinaire Shlomo. Meanwhile, world-class DJs rub shoulders at the festival's cocktail bars, which bustle with activity under the glimmer of starlight and spotlights once the sun goes down.

But The Big Chill's scope reaches well beyond it's diverse musical programme. Venture away from the stages and you'll find a wealth of creativity in many forms. The Words In Motion tent champions the spoken word, while comedians such as Bill Bailey and Dylan Moran play to packed-out tents. The Enchanted Garden provides the perfect place to join in a yoga class, get a massage, or simply lay back in the grass, listening to the festival's non-stop radio station. A diverse film programme entertains audiences of all ages, while the bizarre theatricalities of Punchdrunk, or the Perverse Universe freak show provide thrills for an older crowd. After dark, a variety of visual and interactive art installations bring the woods to life.

But the organisers aren't content to let you rest on your laurels all weekend and audience participation is strongly encouraged in circus workshops, the Village Green Barn Dance, or at any of the numerous Chiller's Spaces that spring up across

page 154 ▶

THE BIGCHILL recommends

Summer Sundae Weekender

De Montfort Hall & Gardens, Granville Road, Leicester

www.summersundae.com

The director of Summer Sundae, Richard Haswell, once said that Supergrass were the perfect act for his festival, and you can see what he means. Fun, friendly, loud and not afraid to speak their mind, Gaz Coombes' gang could hardly be a better fit. It didn't start out that way: the festival was set up in 2001 as an antidote to the big corporate events such as Reading (then the Carling Weekend), which, in those days of yore, held much bigger sway over the summer. With headliners including Morcheeba, Lambchop and Turin Brakes, Summer Sundae went after a cooler, younger, more discerning audience. Now, it has the cachet to bring in the big names – the Streets, the Charlatans, Bon Iver and the Zutons – but still doesn't neglect the little guys.

One thing that sets Summer Sundae apart is its focus on the spoken word, which often gets sidelined at smaller festivals. One of 2008's big surprises, says Haswell, was the poetry tent, Phrased and Confused – 'that was new, and it was a massive hit'. (He has high hopes for the comedy, too: if you can't laugh in a worsening global recession, when can you?)

There's a sense that this is a festival that has outgrown its venue. With BBC Radio 6 as its media partner, Summer Sundae has a level of media coverage that puts most other festivals this size (capacity about 6,000) to shame. But a solution is in sight. Various 'fringe' events have started springing up in Leicester around the festival, with buses provided to ferry punters from one to the next. Many happen on the Thursday night, but this time around they're hoping to schedule gigs as far as two weeks in advance. Keep an eye on summersundaefringe.com for details.

But back to the big event. It's worth noting that it's one of the greener fests, boasting a well-used bike park, and has a strong family-friendly vibe. There's one other thing that gives Summer Sundae the absolute, unbeatable edge over all the rest: if it starts to pour, you can nip inside – into De Montfort Hall, a real, genuine, indoor venue. With a roof and walls and everything. Luxury!
Carrie O'Grady

the site over the course of the weekend, with fun and games including Blind Sheepdog Trials, Snail Racing and croquet on the lawn by the champagne bar.

It's also a place in which families can feel completely at ease. Famous for having the best food of any festival anywhere, at The Big Chill you'll find falafels, doughnuts, burritos, gourmet burgers and a lentil curry to die for. There are children's tents, parades and shows, as well as a small funfair and a huge dressing up box. This is not a place where anyone will tut if your children are getting a little bit boisterous – children are celebrated here, and the organisers clearly drive themselves mad trying to come up with new ways to entertain them every year.

Most of all, people come here to celebrate music, to party and, as you might expect, to chill. It's an event that will leave you with a hatful of images of smiling faces and sunny moments. Spread out in the valley beneath the elegant silhouette of Eastnor castle, with the lake and the woodlands around you, listening to the Singing Dentists, dancing like a loon to Norman Jay's now legendary Sunday afternoon DJ set or sipping a brew at Mr Scruff's Tea Party. Breathing in sweet, fresh Herefordshire air, is all in all, pretty good heaven, and it is absolutely guaranteed that wherever you are, you will, without a shadow of doubt be able to see a stream of bubbles rising into the air, with a small crowd of laughing, leaping festival goers underneath.

Bibi van der Zee

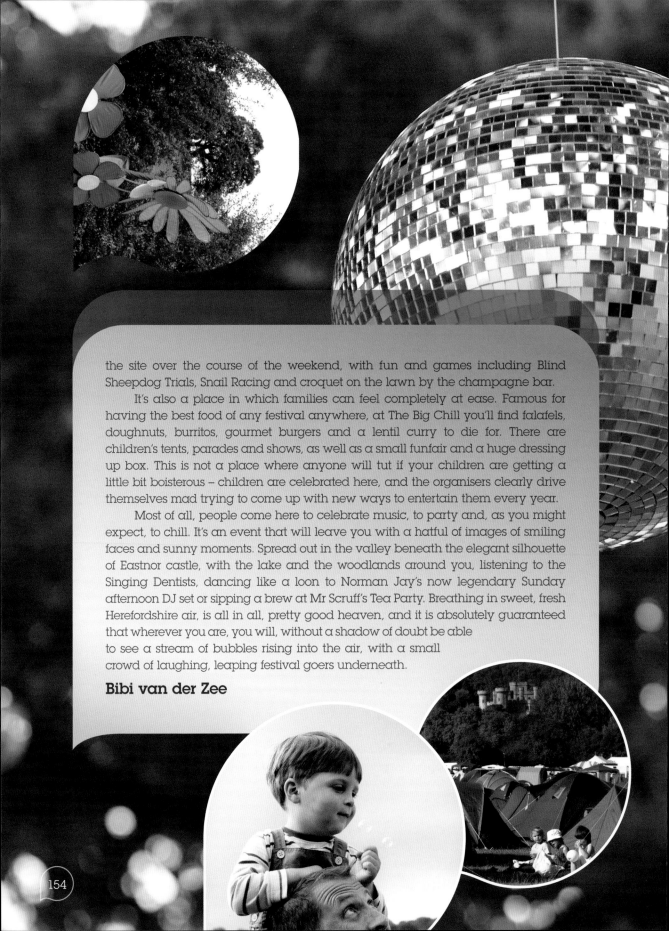

Sticking around

Eastnor and Herefordshire

Now that you've kicked back at the Big Chill, it would be daft not to carry on. Take a few more days to soak up the natural beauty and hospitality that the cider-brewing county of Herefordshire has to offer.

WHERE TO CAMP

The Lucksall caravan and camping park sits on the banks of the beautiful River Wye, so it's not surprising that canoeing and fishing (all equipment available for hire at reception) are staple activities for campers to while away a summer afternoon. Surrounded by countryside, the landlubbers are also catered for. Facilities include a small shop and children's playground.
www.lucksallpark.co.uk

Or, if you feel in need of some luxury after the festival, a break in a yurt or tepee at Little Dewchurch could be the solution.
www.woodlandtipis.co.uk

WHAT TO DO

Walking

It may only be the keenest of ramblers who would take on the full 218km Wye Valley Walk from Chepstow to Plynlimon, through Builth Wells, Hereford and Ross-on-Wye, but for the sheer beauty of varied terrain – gorge, woodland, meadow, orchard and upland – it's well worth taking on a section. The website below suggests shorter loops and linear walks to suit all fitness levels, as well as places of interest to stop along the way.
www.wyevalleywalk.org

Swimming

For an exhilarating swim, it would have to be the River Lugg near Aymestrey where you might be watched by some grazing cows in nearby fields.
www.outdoorswimmingsociety.co.uk

The breathtaking Wye Valley – not bad for a day out.

For the cheekier swimmer, a summer's day dip by the town bridge at Glasbury might find you in the bare-faced company of similarly minded bathers.
www.swimming-holes-wales.org.uk

Wild spot

Haugh Woods, near Woolhope, is one of the best places in the UK to spot butterflies. A designated Site of Special Scientific Interest, over 600 species have been recorded there. Take one of two butterfly trails – suitable for all walkers and wheelchairs in dry weather.
www.wildlifeextra.com/go/uk/haugh-woods.html

After an absence of 300 years, there is increasing evidence that communities of wild boar are once again living in British woodland. With several confirmed sightings near Ross-on-Wye and the Forest of Dean, Herefordshire is one of the best bases in the UK to catch a glimpse. Get advice on some boar-friendly ways to go about it first.
www.britishwildboar.org.uk

We dare you

The wide, meandering River Wye is one of the most popular canoeing locations in the UK, and with good reason. Take a trip with the team at Life-Changing Activities who offer day-long canoe trips. You can think about how it's changing your life during the break for a pub lunch. The guides can help you set personal goals and learn 'what makes you tick' in challenging conditions. More advanced canoeing trips including rapids are also available.
www.lifechangingactivities.com

Stroll into the past in the pretty market town of Ledbury.

If it rains

The Hereford cider museum is stuffed with collections of all things drink-related – cider presses, casks, vats and exotic drinking implements. For scholars of cider, there's a research library. All that learning will be thirsty work – so head to the distillery to sample some of the county's best cider apple brandy.
www.cidermuseum.co.uk

If you fancy more sober entertainment, you could put your creative energies to the test at Eastnor Pottery, in the estate of Eastnor Castle. A brilliant stress-relieving activity, there are workshops for adults or children.
www.eastnorpottery.co.uk

FOOD AND DRINK

Beer

Westons Cider Company, based in the village of Much Marcle for 125 years, offers tours around the mill. You can see how cider goes from orchard to pint glass. Adults will be kept busy with the cider

and perry tasting, while kids can run about in an adventure playground or go for dray horse rides. If happen to be on your bike, you could try a cycling/tasting tour around a number of producers.
www.westons-cider.co.uk; www.ciderroute.co.uk/site/ciderCycling.html

Wine

The Coddington vineyard near Ledbury was planted in 1985 on the site of an old cider orchard. It's a small, family-run business producing award-winning wines from three varieties of grape, including pinot gris. It's also set in charming surrounds with a beautiful garden, stream and carp pond. Open for tours and tastings most months of the year.
www.coddingtonvineyard.com

On a much larger scale is the vineyard at Broadfield Court, Bodenham. The estate produces six different types of wine.
www.broadfieldcourt.co.uk

For more information about other Herefordshire wineries visit
www.herefordshirelife.co.uk/food-and-drink-a-tasting-tour-of-hereford's-vineyards--105540

Local produce

At the Monkland dairy at Pleck Farm you can see cheese being made to original Herefordshire specifications, sample the award-winning yellow stuff, or sit down and have a pint and ploughman's in the cafe.
www.mousetrapcheese.co.uk

Sample some delicious ice-cream made with ewes' milk – only 7% fat – in charming surroundings.
www.shepherdsicecream.co.uk

FOR THE KIDS

There are few cuter creatures than a miniature pony – except maybe a miniature donkey or goat. The kids will love the Small Breeds Farm Park and Owl Centre (they may not be the only ones), and let's not get started on the baby miniature animals you might find there. The owl centre offers a unique opportunity to view rare and endangered species and learn about their conservation.
www.owlcentre.com

A rather cute Soay sheep at the Small Breeds Farm Park.

august

Make the most of the month

Dip and whirl

Kites from Spain, China, Switzerland and Tasmania fill the skies at Portsmouth's annual kite festival, which has been running since 1992. Those on show include soft models in the shape of flowers or animals, stunt kites such as the Revolution that can perform all sorts of tricks, artistic cellular creations and appliquéd flyers. Most people can only take a couple of hours of craning their neck backwards and a lack of wind can scupper the whole event. But in a good year, it's one of the most amazing spectacles you can imagine.
www.portsmouthkitefestival.org.uk

Joust

In the architectural glory years of Queen Anne's reign, the first Duke of Marlborough, having defeated the French in some battle or other, was given a tonne of public money to build Blenheim Palace. The result, in the hills of Oxfordshire, was something grand and imposing enough for any Brit to take pride in, and in August you can picnic on its lawns while watching medieval jousting, archery and falconry. Bring food good enough for such gorgeous surroundings – a roasted suckling pig would probably not be out of place.
www.blenheimpalace.com

Bike

The Tarka Trail in north Devon offers 30 miles of gorgeous countryside from Braunton through Barnstaple, Bideford and Torrington before finishing in Meeth. Make sure you stop at the beautiful pannier market in Barnstaple – on market days this still bristles with high-quality fruit and vegetables, and the nearby shops are stuffed with mouth-watering local produce. The Yarde Orchard cafe, one of the best refuelling stops on the trail, also offers a bunkhouse if you don't think you can go a mile further. The Cyclists' Breakfast – made with local organic eggs, bacon and sausages - is lauded far and wide and will keep you pedalling for quite a few miles.
www.devon.gov.uk/tarkatrail; www.yarde-orchard.co.uk

Party

Everyone must go to the Notting Hill Carnival at least once in their lives: it may not be quite the Rio Carnival, but it's Europe's largest street party, complete with the obligatory wee in someone's front garden and dance at your favourite sound system. The first day on Sunday is family day – things are a little more tranquil and it's easier to move around. By Monday, the party has cranked up: it can take two hours to get down one street and you'll find that the group you were due to meet on the corner have moved to another sound system. You just have to roll with it, samba along and make sure you enjoy every minute.
www.nottinghillcarnival.biz

Applaud

If, for some reason, you need an excuse to spend a couple of days beside the sea watching boats whipping back and forth in a competitive and entertaining fashion, then the Whitby Regatta in Yorkshire is it. Claiming to be the oldest sea regatta in England, the event is not just confined to the water, but includes aerial displays, a parade through town, children's entertainment such as Punch and Judy, and a motorbike gymkhana. To round it all off, there's a stupendous firework display over St Hilda's Abbey, which hangs over the small town.
www.whitbyregatta.co.uk

Scoff

The Summer Isles hotel in the very north-west of Scotland opens only for the summer months; it is famed throughout the area for its seafood, which is almost all caught locally and whisked straight into the restaurant kitchen. Freshly baked brown bread, eggs from local hens, or wonderful Scottish and English cheeses all accompany the award-winning seafood. To top it off, the restaurant looks over the bay towards the Summer Isles and beyond to the Hebrides. A seafood-lover's dream.
www.summerisleshotel.co.uk

Spectate

It is hard to believe that just off the Strand in London, a short walk from the chaos of Trafalgar Square, you can relax beneath the stars (such as they are in the capital's centre) and watch a movie. Every summer Somerset House hangs up a huge screen in its neo-classical courtyard and holds a little film season. Screenings in 2008 included work by Fellini, Kubrick and Guillermo del Toro. Bring along a cushion or a blanket, plus someone to hold hands with, and forget the city exists.
www.somersethouse.org.uk/film

Bake

Andrew Whitley is a bread evangelist. For more than 30 years he has been baking his wonderful loaves and trying to remind the rest of us what true bread is like – without additives, improvers, colours or flavourings. In the process, he has seen a fantastic renaissance in the noble art of baking and those of you who are now fatally addicted to real bread may want to spend a weekend with the master baker. He is based in Cumbria near the Village Bakery, the company he founded. Pain de campagne, Russian-style ryes, 'Cromarty cob' and even the greatest challenge of all, the true sourdough: Whitley can turn his hand to any style of bread and will help you learn how to do it too.
www.breadmatters.com

Stroll

Wait for a quiet and mellow afternoon, then head to Surrey to visit Hannah Peschar's sculpture garden. For more than 20 years, Peschar has been exhibiting artworks integrated into the greenery in this magical 10-acre site. As you meander through copses and take footbridges over ponds in the dappled light, with the lovely smell of fern and woodland around you, the artworks almost sing.
www.hannahpescharsculpture.com

Giggle

There are many imitators but no true competitors: the Edinburgh festival is the largest arts festival in the world. In a good year you may find a ballet about Dorian Gray, a site-specific recreation of an office party, a one-man piece about Palestine, a Polish puppet show inspired by Jorge Luis Borges and a two-hander set in a France ravaged by the plague – all on at 10am and performing to an audience of one. It's pure lunacy in the best possible way.

But how on earth do you navigate this maze of shows and find something worth seeing? In 2008, there were more than 2,000 events at 250 venues with the book, television, fringe and international festivals all running side by side.
It's a fruit machine, really, but start with the big four venues – Gilded Balloon, Pleasance, Assembly Rooms and Underbelly – then read the papers, listen to gossip and try to track down the teeny little show somewhere in the outer darkness that will be the surprise smash hit of the festival. Some years it's lemons, but others, it's cherries all the way.
www.edbookfest.co.uk; www.mgeitf.co.uk/home/mgeitf.aspx; www.edfringe.com; www.eif.co.uk

Bibi van der Zee

Summer

Uninvited guests

There are some countries – Australia springs to mind

– in which every living creature from the smallest spider to the largest mammal has been designed to kill a person at 20 paces. Those who are nervous about being around animals should be thankful therefore, that Britain is not one of those countries. The chances of coming to any sort of grief by dint of some unfortunate interaction are very slim indeed. The following guidance, however, can help if you do find yourself in an awkward situation.

Cattle

Call it a result of our overly urbanised society, but many people needlessly frighten themselves by mistaking cows for bulls. Before terror strikes, check if those bulls have udders. Cows are generally very peace-loving creatures and pay little attention to humans beyond a bemused gaze. However, they have a strong maternal instinct and are very protective of their offspring, so if you are passing through a field with cows and calves in it, avoid walking between the two.

It's a myth that bulls are attracted to the colour red, but they do become disturbed by excessive movement. Therefore, the best course of action to take if you come across bulls is to make a path around them unobtrusively as possible. Should a bull start towards you, move away calmly and do not try to outrun it. On most occasions it will stop before it reaches you. If it shows no signs of doing so, turn to face it, step towards it and wave your arms, shouting fiercely and letting it know who is boss. Once it does, continue to make a measured exit.

Farmers are only legally allowed to keep bulls up to 10 months old in fields crossed by public footpaths. Beyond this age, bulls from dairy breeds are banned, while all other bulls can only be kept in such fields if cows or heifers (young cows) are present. However, if any bull acts in a way that seriously endangers anyone

iving

Highland cattle: a cow (left) and a bull (right). Spot the difference!

using a footpath, the incident should be reported to the landowner, the police and the Ramblers' Association (www.ramblers.org.uk, 0207 339 8500).

Highland cattle, though fearsome to look at with their shaggy brown coats and don't-mess-with-me horns, are actually one of Britain's more docile breeds, though it is still wise not to take them on.

Snakes

Britain has just one native poisonous snake: the adder. It rarely strikes out unless provoked and even then its bite is unlikely to be fatal (there have been just 14 deaths in Britain since 1876). You are more likely to encounter entirely harmless grass snakes or slow worms, of which there is no need to be fearful. Should the worst happen and you are bitten by an adder (identifiable by the 'V' on its head and chevrons running down its back), do not try to suck out the venom, John Wayne-style, since this will only spread the poison. Do not touch the wound or attempt to apply a tourniquet. Rather, stay as still and calm as possible (to prevent your blood from pumping the poison around your body too rapidly), take a paracetamol if you're in pain, and get someone to whisk you to a hospital quick sharp, where you will be treated with antivenin.

Horses

These are normally very placid beasts whose interest in bipeds only runs to whether they happen to be carrying a stash of sugar cubes. However, they can kick out if spooked by sudden noise or movement (especially just behind them), so move slowly and calmly in their presence, giving them a wide berth, and all should be well.

Dogs

There's nothing scarier than a dog tearing towards you with its jaws slathering and its demon-possessed eyes rapidly sizing up the most vulnerable points of your body. If you can't escape its attentions by nimbly scaling a nearby fence, the best course of action is to demonstrate that you are not a threat to it. Stand absolutely still, facing the dog but without making eye contact (which the dog will interpret as confrontational). Keep your hands in your pockets and wait for the dog to leave, or move away slowly and as smoothly as you can.

Wasps

If you find your picnic plagued by wasps, cover up anything sugary, including fizzy drinks. Put some fruit juice or, if you can find it, rotting fruit, into a bowl or cup and place it a safe distance from your picnic. The wasps will swiftly move on to the decoy. Just in case you're the sort of person who takes such things on picnics, it's worth noting that this trick also works with opened tins of cat food.

Dixe Wills

Summer

Cloud-watching

Dante claimed that the only perfect view was the one of the sky above our heads. Gazing dreamily up at the heavens on a warm summer's day, there are few who would argue with him. However, if the sky were merely a wide expanse of cerulean emptiness, we would soon get bored. It's the clouds that give the firmament its character, seeming to be always on the move while remaining calm and at peace (we'll overlook their occasional temper tantrum).

If you want to go from merely admiring clouds to a better understanding of them, the first thing to learn is that there are three basic types: cumulus, stratus and cirrus. Between them they form seven further common types – stratocumulus, altocumulus, cirrocumulus, cumulonimbus, nimbostratus, altostratus and cirrostratus. This may seem a baffling jumble of Latin initially, but with a little practice, you'll soon be confidently sorting your altocumulus from your cirrostratus and wondering how you ever got them confused.

Cumulus

The five members of the cumulus group are easily identifiable because they are all composed of one or more clearly defined lumps of cloud (cumulus being the Latin word for 'heap'). A straight **cumulus** cloud is the most stereotypical of the lot – a big fluffy wad of candyfloss as seen in countless children's drawings of the sky. It is also known as the 'fair weather cloud' because it glides across summer skies without bringing a sniff of rain.

Stratocumulus, meanwhile, is a mass of low cumulus clouds joined together. White or grey in colour, any rain they might bring will only be light. **Altocumulus** clouds prefer neither to hit the heights nor slum it in the depths with stratocumulus. They don't bear rain and often form a layer mid-sky of what seems to be scores of cotton wool balls loosely attached to one another. **Cirrocumulus**, on the other hand, is a very high flyer (about 20,000ft, as opposed to 2,000ft for stratocumulus

chilling

and 6,500+ft for altocumulus). Its tufts of white or light blue cloud create a ripple or 'mackerel' effect.

There is no mistaking **cumulonimbus** – the archetypal storm cloud and largest member of the cumulus family. It appears as a dense mass piling itself up into the sky like a giant anvil. Often dark, cumulonimbus brings strong winds and heavy rain or hail (or snow in winter), and is sometimes accompanied by thunder and lightning.

A dramatic cumulonimbus cloud ready to do its thing.

(Clockwise from top): puffy cumulus, mackerel cirrocumulus, dark blanket altostratus and (behind) wispy cirrus

Stratus

The four stratus clouds are best thought of as wet blankets. They're responsible for those days when everything looks grim and a huge portion of the sky – or all of it – is blotted out by a spreading, almost featureless, mass. It still doesn't mean you can't grow to love them, of course.

Stratus itself is easy to spot: it's basically fog, only higher up. Not much higher up, mind – at its most depressed it can descend to cover the tops of electricity pylons. **Altostratus** is much the same thing, only at a higher altitude (6,500+ft). Both can bring drizzle, though you'd have to be up a mountain and inside an altostratus cloud to get wet. **Cirrostratus**, meanwhile, is so high (20,000ft) that the water it holds becomes ice crystals, which can be all but invisible from ground level. If a blue sky takes on a slightly milky sheen, it's possible that this is what you're actually seeing. **Nimbostratus**, however, is a very different creature. Much of the rain, sleet and snow you have ever had fall on you will have dropped from these dark mantles of cloud, the undersides of which are conventionally tatty and torn. If you experience any prolonged period of rain, you can be pretty sure that it comes courtesy of nimbostratus.

Cirrus

Cirrus clouds are wispy, feathery and high in the sky. There are three different types: **cirrus** itself, cirrocumulus and cirrostratus. The latter two are also members of the cumulus and stratus groups respectively and are described above. Cirrus, like cirrostratus, is made of ice crystals. However, it tends to be more substantial than its cousin, forming long, downy threads that trail across the sky.

Contrails

These are the high thin lines caused by the water vapour emitted from airplane engines. When the exhaust cools, condensation forms and a white streak is left across the sky. Are they proper clouds? The decision is all yours.

Further clouding

Of course, there's more complexity in the world of clouds than we've covered here. There are, for instance, 14 cloud species determined by their shape and structure, and nine varieties that deal with their arrangement and transparency. But none of this need concern you when, more interestingly, you've spotted a cloud the shape of a cat chasing another that looks like a mouse ...

Dixe Wills

Fooling a

Flirting

It's the old, familiar story. Your eyes meet across a crowded tent … and then unmeet as 200 ecstatic dancers, dazzling disco lights and your own intoxication get in the way of the instant bond you formed with a total stranger. But fear not – festivals, whether musical, gastronomical, sporting or otherwise, are the perfect place for flirting. The drink is flowing, the sun is shining (with luck), the clothing is minimal and there's a general air of benevolence to all mankind that's impossible to resist. It's no coincidence that the song you hear most often at the Big Chill is John Paul Young's easygoing AOR classic, Love Is in the Air.

That said, the very nature of festivals can make it hard to hook up. Many are now family-friendly, attracting couples rather than big groups of single lads and lasses – there may be a lot of pouting and cuddling going on in the Kids Tent or Club Mum, but it won't be the adults who are doing it. The big groups can be discouraging, too; nothing kills confidence like being snickered at by a chorus of strangers who are watching you try it on with their best mate. And even if you do connect with someone you like the look of, arranging to meet them later is fraught with pitfalls. Many a potentially great relationship has been nipped in the bud with the words, 'I'll see you later – somewhere around the main stage.'

But dedicated flirters always find a way. The Big Chill has been known to host speed-dating sessions at the Big Romance, and for five years the Guardian's Soulmates dating service ran a matchmaking tent in conjunction with Greenpeace at Glastonbury, with games, prizes and a chatting area. The organiser recalls one memorable game of Blind Date in which the three blokes, blindfolded, were unaware that their interrogator was completely naked – had been for three days, in fact. 'She was very eldritch, a bit of a hippie,' says the Guardian staffer. 'The lad was thrilled to bits when he found out.'

If that sounds a little too full-on to suit your style, mock weddings and druidic "handfasting" ceremonies are a lovely way to make your feelings known. In 2006 Lost Vagueness brought their Chapel of Love and Loathing to the Big Chill, hosting a mass wedding that saw everyone from women in suspender-belts to lifelong

round

lovers tie the knot. The Inflatable Church at Bestival holds weddings every half an hour, to the sweet strains of Primal Scream's Movin' On Up. Jake Shears of Scissor Sisters was one of the grooms (or brides?); he married himself, in the form of a mirror. Some people take it even further: one Leicestershire man married his bride for real at Download in Donington, the hard-rockers' festival of choice. Their cake was in the shape of a big bass drum, complete with logo.

One girl's story didn't pan out quite so well. She arrived at Glastonbury with her boyfriend but ended up having a fling with a mutual friend. Cue much sneaking off to 'get beers' or 'go back to the tent for some stuff I forgot'. Finally she left the festival with her boyfriend, secretly relieved that she had got away with it. But she and the other boy must have made a good couple, because several weeks later, she was appalled to see their photo on the cover of NME – they epitomised the spirit of Glasto love. Her boyfriend, when he saw it, did not share in that spirit.

Mostly, though, festival flirtations have a happy ending. 'Everyone went away with a smile on their face,' recalls the Soulmates staffer – even if they didn't make a match. With most people in daft costumes and several drinks to the good, it's no surprise that there are innumerable stories of proposals. At the Big Chill in 2004, one young hopeful got a plane to fly over the site, trailing a banner that read: 'Bog Will you marry me? Love Whip X.' Before you ask, she said yes, and the couple married – at Eastnor Castle, naturally – the following year. Bog, aka Louise, remembers the day: 'We had most of the field come and congratulate us. Many were in tears with us, which was very sweet – we all cried in unison.'

Top tips

● Do smile and be silly. No point playing hard-to-get or sophisticated in this sort of atmosphere; you'll only come across as a killjoy.

● Do get some hardcore flirting done on the first evening if you can. It's the only time your hair is going to look halfway decent.

● Do go to see bands you love and single out the person there who obviously loves them as much as you do – a perfect talking point.

● Do hang around the backstage area and flirt with artists if you can. Gives you instant cred at work on Monday morning.

● Don't get too bladdered. You might make a date for the next day and forget all about it – and standing someone up is just plain rude.

● Don't rely on your mobile. Too many users + too few masts = radio silence.

● Don't stalk. If someone is backing away from you, alarmed, then let them go with grace.

● Girls – bring a compact, the old-fashioned kind with a mirror and powder-puff. If you've got mud on your cheek, it's easier to get it off when you can see it, and besides you'll look cute dabbing the puff around your nose.

● Guys – avoid overuse of deodorant, spray, aftershave, anything artificial. Good, honest sweat is much more of a turn-on than gallons of cheap perfume.

● Gays – don't just stick to the Pink Zones. There are a lot of curious people out there, and their inhibitions have never been lower.

Carrie O'Grady

Festival People

James Hervey-Bathurst
The Big Chill's landlord

My family has lived in Eastnor Castle, near the town of Ledbury in Herefordshire, for nearly 200 years, and it's been open to the public for much of that time. We've held all sorts of events here: a Jools Holland concert, weddings, outdoor theatre, a hobby and model fair and corporate functions. My grandfather held a huge scout jamboree in 1937. It's what we do – we're in the business of leisure and entertainment.

But the Big Chill is of a different order. In 2003, the first year they were here, about 10,000 people attended and now there are about 30,000. I'm full of admiration for the way it's managed: their organisation seems to get better every year.

The money they pay us goes to the maintenance of the estate because each year there are different things that need doing, such as mending roofs, planting trees, converting redundant buildings and so on. You don't let it get you down and you make sure that the repairs are long-term. You only want to mend the castle roof once every hundred years. And, of course, these things don't detract from the pleasure of living here.

It's one of the big questions: what can we do in the countryside to earn money? Farming, of course, and a bit of tourism, but Herefordshire is not really a huge tourist destination. So an event that brings 30,000 people into the area gives locals a chance to make a better living for that period. Anything that helps bring people to our part of the world is good.

The park is a magical place in the summer. The festival isn't held near the sensitive area, where the rare butterflies are, but in the woodland pasture, so it doesn't really affect the wildlife. But beautiful places need maintaining: oak trees die, roads wear out, fences fall down. Some parts of the countryside are wild, naturally beautiful, but in this part of the world, the countryside needs maintaining and this gives us the means to keep going.

So when we heard that the Big Chill organisers were looking for a venue we got in touch with them straight away. We like these sort of events and the Big Chill had very good references from its previous venue.

I like taking my kids up there – it's just under a mile from home. I like some of the headliners – Lily Allen, Leonard Cohen – but I don't get in to see many of the others. I'm more of a classical person, but I love the atmosphere even if I don't really get pop music. I love to see all these people having a great time, families enjoying themselves with the Malvern Hills in the background. It really is chilled.

One of my best moments occurred when Cohen was performing. He just sang, didn't talk that much, and there was an incredible atmosphere in the crowd. It was very moving. Someone in front of me had on a T-shirt with the places his tour had gone – Moscow, Geneva, Rome. At the bottom of the list was Ledbury.

www.eastnorcastle.com

Dish of the

Goan fish curry

From Big Chill regulars the Goan Seafood Company

THE GOAN
SEAFOOD CO.

Serves 4

Ingredients:

4 tbsp sunflower oil

2 large onions, finely chopped

3 large cloves garlic, crushed or grated

1 inch fresh ginger, finely grated

1 tbsp coriander seeds (ground)

1 tbsp cumin seeds (ground)

1 tsp turmeric

1–2 tsp chilli powder (adjust to taste)

1 tsp salt (adjust to taste)

1kg pollack fillet, skinned, with the tiny pin bones removed, and cut into bite-size pieces (you could substitute any firm white fish)

2 tbsp tamarind water or 1 tsp tamarind concentrate

2 x 400g tins chopped tomatoes

Handful fresh coriander, chopped

Chopped fresh chillies (optional)

Method:

- Fry the onions, garlic and ginger in the oil until soft but not coloured. Add the spices and salt, and cook for a minute or two. (We always grind whole spices just before using. You can use ready-ground spices but you won't get the same fresh flavour.) Add the tamarind water (or concentrate) and the chopped tomatoes. Bring to boil and simmer for 15–20 minutes until it looks well combined.

- You can make the sauce in advance to this point and then refrigerate (or freeze) until required.

- Bring the sauce to the boil, add the fish and cook gently for a couple of minutes until just cooked through (don't overcook it). Add the coriander (and chillies if you want extra heat) and serve immediately with basmati rice.

Drink of th

Dark and stormy

From the Big Chill bartenders

Pour the ingredients (except ginger beer) into a glass, **add** ice, **cover** and **shake**. Add a little more ice if necessary and **top up** with ginger beer. **Garnish** with a lime wedge.

15ml fresh lime juice
5ml sugar syrup
2 splashes Angostura
  bitters
50ml gold or dark rum
Ginger beer

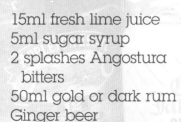

e month

Game of

Sheepdog trials

This is one for those with big families

or lots of friends to entertain. Get into teams of five or six and see who has, and who hasn't, got what it takes to make it as a sheepdog.

Each team must elect one person to be their leader, or 'sheepdog'. It's best to choose someone with good co-ordination and lots of patience for this role – it's not easy to herd the rest of the group around a course involving a number of set challenges. Especially when you can talk to them, but not touch them. And especially when they're blindfolded.

Before the trials can begin, decide on the five or so tasks each team must attempt and plot the course. Use what's around you — you could get the sheepdog to herd their group down a path without anyone stepping off it, circle a tree without bumping into it or get over

a fence without falling. Alternatively, devise your own tests with any bits and bobs you have to hand. Mark out a pen on the ground and have the sheepdog try to shepherd their team into it, or build an obstacle course with deck chairs and picnic tables. Don't make anything too tricky, though – even the simplest tasks become tremendously difficult when you can't see anything. Points are awarded for each challenge successfully completed and, if there is a draw, the group with the fastest time takes the title.

Want to make the trials even more interesting? Ban talking and give each sheepdog a whistle.

Carrie O'Grady

August festival directory

MUSIC

BIG ONES

The Big Chill
When: Early August
Where: Eastnor Castle, Great Malvern, Herefordshire
Cost: £129 adult, £60 13-15, under 13s free
Website: www.bigchill.net
The kind of vibe that will get under the skin of the most jaded festival goer. Genuinely chilled out, grown up partying that started life as a shindig in Islington and still manages to be relaxed even with crowds of 30,000.

Reading/Leeds Festivals
When: Late August
Where: Richfield Avenue, Reading and Bramham Park, near Leeds
Cost: £165 per weekend camping ticket
Website: www.leedsfestival.com; www.readingfestival.com
The southern half of this simultaneous festival has a stellar rock and indie heritage – Nirvana and the Stone Roses both played their last UK gigs there. Don't be surprised if the nice man next to you starts lobbing plastic bottles at the band. It's a Reading tradition.

V Festival
When: Late August
Where: Hylands Park, Chelmsford and Weston Park, Staffordshire
Cost: £155 for weekend ticket including camping
Website: www.vfestival.com

Offers a good mix-up of the year's biggest rock, pop and indie names – the V stands for Virgin, so expect things to be at the more commercial end of the spectrum. Ideal if you like your festivals without the rough edges.

ROCK/INDIE

Beachdown Festival
When: Late August
Where: Devils Dyke, South Downs, East Sussex
Cost: £85 for weekend
Website: www.beachdownfestival.com
The Brighton vibe, captured in four days of eclectic music, film and comedy. No need to pack your wellies though. The chalk base of the South Downs location sucks rainwater away, so no mud.

Bloodstock Open Air
When: Mid August
Where: Catton Hall, Walton-on-Trent, South Derbyshire
Cost: Around £90 including camping, children £35
Website: www.bloodstock.uk.com
Mmm, the smell of sweaty leather and the sound of thousands of metal heads rocking out in what is usually a sleepy Derbyshire village. Mixing up established and unsigned acts, expect three days of metal mayhem.

Bulldog Bash
When: Early August
Where: Shakespeare County Raceway, Long Marston, Warwickshire.
Cost: Adult around £55.
Website: www.bulldogbash.eu
A festival by bikers, for bikers was never

going to be ordinary. If you like the sound of topless car washing (really), live wrestling and a Run What Ya Brung dragstrip, this could be your idea of heaven. If not, then definitely not.

Creation Festival
When: Mid August
Where: Royal Cornwall Showground, Wadebridge, Cornwall
Cost: Free
Website: www.creationfest.org.uk
Six and a half thousand believers getting on down at the UK's largest Christian music festival. After you've been to the massive skatepark, take in a bible lesson. Goes without saying, this one is family friendly.

Endorse-It In-Dorset
When: Early August
Where: Sixpenny Handley, Cranborne Chase, Dorset
Cost: Adult around £75
Website: www.lgofestivals.com
Keeping it real in rural Dorset this is a proper homegrown affair with a line-up to match. The venue sounds like something out of Beatrix Potter and it's managed to stay free of corporate sponsorship. Old school festivaling.

Get Loaded in the Park
When: Late August
Where: Clapham Common, south London
Cost: Around £35 per ticket
Website: www.getloadedinthepark.com
Love festivals, hate camping? Here you go. Dance your urban socks off to big indie and dance acts then hop on the tube home. We can't guarantee the portaloos won't have that special festival pong though.

Hydro Connect
When: Late August
Where: Inveraray Castle, Argyll, Scotland
Cost: £140 adult, £70 child
Website: www.connectmusicfestival.com
Never mind the music, check out the setting. A fairytale castle nestled on the heather-clad banks of a loch, anyone? Headline acts like Bjork, Duffy, Elbow and Franz Ferdinand

have all done battle with the scenery and lost.

Rebellion UK
When: Early August
Where: The Wintergardens, Blackpool, Lancashire
Cost: Weekend ticket in the region of £65
Website: www.rebellionfestivals.com
An indoor festival, so no danger of your Mohawk wilting in the rain. Four thousand punks descending on Blackpool may sound scary but worry not. There's Punk Rock Bingo for the more sedate. Aw.

Retrofest
When: Late August
Where: Strathclyde Country Park, North Lanarkshire, Scotland
Cost: Around £80 adult weekend (£95 camping), Child (under 13) weekend £40 (£47.50 camping)
Website: www.retrofest.co.uk
Dust off your batwing jumpers, crack open the Sun-In and go back in time. This is one big stage and all your old favourites. Think Rick Astley, ABC and Showaddywaddy and you're on the right lines.

Solfest
When: Late
Where: West Cumbria
Cost: £80 adult, £15 child
Website: www.solwayfestival.co.uk
Refreshingly focused on creating a proper festival vibe rather than squeezing every penny out of you, pints are at pub prices and music ranges from your Roisin Murphys to Chas and Dave.

Standon Calling
When: Early August
Where: Ware, Hertfordshire
Cost: Tickets around £70
Website: www.standon-calling.com
A small, theatrical indie fest – headliners in 2008 included Super Furry Animals and Mystery Jets – expect surprise events, secret areas and fantastical folk popping up to direct your partying. For the camping-phobic

Hit me with your rhythm stick and go morris mad at Broadstairs.

there are candy coloured beach huts (sheds, but hey, they're dry).

Summer Sundae Weekender

When: Early August
Where: De Montfort Hall, Leicester
Cost: Adult weekend tickets between £95-£159
Website: www.summersundae.com
A festival with some spit and polish, expect high production values, nice clean bars and loos, and apparently you can even stand right up by the main stage without having your ribs crushed. How civilised.

Underage

When: Early August
Where: Victoria Park, London
Cost: Tickets are £23
Website: www.underagefestivals.com
What do you get when you put 7,500 teenagers in a field for nine hours, the likes of Dizzee Rascal on stage and decree strictly no parents allowed? The world's first credible, teens-only festival of course. Oh, and a whole lot of raging hormones.

FOLK

Beautiful Days

When: Mid/Late August
Where: Escot Park, near Fairmile, Devon
Cost: Around £90 for the weekend
Website: www.beautifuldays.org
Don't expect corporate sponsors or big brands – this is a festival brought to you by anarchist rockers the Levellers, after all. Do expect an authentic vibe and great music from the likes of Squeeze and Nouvelle Vague.

Belladrum Tartan Heart Festival

When: Early August
Where: Belladrun Estate, Inverness-shire, Scotland
Cost: Weekend tickets around £80; Saturday £50; children (12 and under) Free
Website: www.tartanheartfestival.co.uk
The Scots know how to party and this grassroots affair is Highland magic with a hip

edge. Previous headliners include Lee Scratch Perry and Biffy Clyro.

Broadstairs Folk Week

When: Early-Mid August
Where: Various venues Broadstairs, Kent
Cost: Adult season ticket around £145, events individually priced
Website: www.broadstairsfolkweek.org.uk
Ah, the sweet sound of folk learning to play penny whistles, ukuleles, banjos and accordions. Chuck on some big wooden shoes and do the Appalachian Clog. A rabble-rousing carnival atmosphere.

Fairport Convention's Cropred

When: Early August
Where: Cropredy, nr Banbury, Oxfordshire
Cost: £72 plus £30 for camping
Website: www.fairportconcention.com
Pitch up in a canal boat if you don't fancy camping, get brekkie at the village hall and watch the legendary folk rockers themselves take on the village at cricket. There's music too, of course.

Farmer Phil's Festival

When: Mid August
Where: Ratlinghope, Shropshire
Cost: Around £50 weekend ticket including camping
Website: www.farmerphilsfestival.co.uk
When you learn that Farmer Phil (yes, he does exist) built the festival's revolving stage from an eight-cow rotary milking parlour carousel, you start to get a feel for this quirky annual festival. A real one-off.

Green Man Festival

When: Early/Mid August
Where: Glanusk Park, Crickhowell, Dowys
Cost: Tickets £105, under 12s free
Website: www.thegreenmanfestival.co.uk
Mist rolling in off the river, ancient trees strung with lights, Brecon Beacons as a backdrop to the main stage. Oh, and the only UK festival with 24-hour bars which fund this resolutely non-corporate favourite.

The Moor Music Festival

When: Early August
Where: Near Ilkley, West Yorkshire
Cost: Adult tickets around £60, £20 teen ticket
Website: www.moormusicfestival.co.uk
If you find yourself on Ilkla Moor Baht'at*, make tracks to this homely, not-for-profit festival that manages to attract class acts like Utah Saints and the Jamie Finlay Band. (*That's 'without a hat' in case you're wondering).

Pontardawe Festival

When: Mid August
Where: Parc Ynysderw, Pontardawe Leisure Centre, Ffordd Parc Ynysderw, Pondarwe, Swansea.
Cost: Adult around £60
Website: www.pontardawefestival.com
Folksy world music and Celtic foot stomping in the Swansea Valley, with a fringe festival in the village. Only now recovering its strength after rain and foot and mouth all but brought it to its knees in 2001.

Shrewsbury Folk Festival

When: Late August
Where: Shrewsbury Showground, Shrewsbury, Shropshire
Cost: Season ticket around £90. Full day tickets available. Kids half price. Camping £12 extra.
Website: www.shrewsburyfolkfestival.co.uk
Wave your hankies in the air like you don't care. Yes, this is your chance to learn how to Morris dance, whirl about at a ceilidh or sing along to the likes of the Proclaimers. Good family fun.

Tapestry Goes West

When: Early August
Where: Margam Park, Port Talbot
Cost: Around £60
Website: www.tapestrygoeswest.com
Underground London club takes itself off to Wales to inject some medieval frolics into the festival circuit. Organisers claim it's all about the bands but come on, there's jousting people.

DANCE/ELECTRONICA

Creamfields

When: Late August
Where: Daresbury, Cheshire
Cost: Weekend around £115, £60 day
Website: www.creamfields.com
Arguably 'the' big dance event of the summer – 65,000 clubbers can't be wrong – previous line-ups include Fatboy Slim, the Chemical Brothers, Goldfrapp and Basement Jaxx.

Field Day

When: Early August
Where: Victoria Park, east London
Cost: Around £30
Website: www.fielddayfestivals.com
Turning an urban dance music festival into a country fete probably doesn't get the stamp of approval from the Countryside Alliance but who cares. Enter a carrot eating contest, have a dance. Wang a welly, have a dance. You get the idea.

The Magic Loungeabout

When: Late August
Where: Newburgh Priory, Yorkshire
Cost: Adult around £80, children free
Website: www.themagicloungeabout.net
For those who like their electronic music festivals with a bit more luxury, dahling. Free yurts, breakfast in bed, sofas in the beer tents, champagne cocktails, Gary Numan, that kind of thing.

Shambala

When: End August
Where: Kelmarsh, Northampton
Cost: Adult around £80, £25 child
Website: www.shambalafestival.org
A free spirit of the festival circuit, with its tongue firmly in its cheek, this is a big fat rave held at a secret location. Four days of loveliness, fancy dress, hot tubs and dancing...lots of dancing.

CLASSICAL/JAZZ

Brecon Jazz
When: Early August
Where: Venues around Brecon town
Cost: Events individually priced
Website: www.breconjazz.co.uk
The recent on/off saga seems finally to be over. The 25 year-old festival is officially back on but scaled down, so international jazzmeisters can once again take over a corner of mid Wales.

INTERNATIONAL

FM4 Frequency Festival
When: Mid-late August
Where: Salzburgring, Austria
Cost: Adults around £70
Website: www.frequency.at
A big, mainstream rock festival, recent line-ups have included Kaiser Chiefs, Morrissey and Muse, along with less well-known (in the UK anyway) German and Austrian names. Hasselhoff fans should look elsewhere.

Lollapalooza
When: Early August
Where: Grant Park, Chicago, US
Tickets: Around $190 for a 3 day pass
Website: www.lollapalooza.com
Big, brash and chockful of corporate sponsorship this is not one for the fainthearted but the brave will be rewarded with a mind-boggling line-up. Practically every band you've ever heard of will be playing.

Lowlands
When: Mid August
Where: Biddinghuizen, the Netherlands
Cost: 150 euros for weekend including camping
Website: www.lowlands.nl
Progressive outdoor festivalling the Dutch way, which means most of the stages are sensibly under canvas, expect big names – Arctic Monkeys, Bon Iver etc – and extras like its own daily newspaper and currency.

Angels, devils and everything in between at the Edinburgh Fringe.

Sziget

When: Mid August
Where: Óbudai Island, Budapest, Hungary
Cost: 150 euros per ticket including camping
Website: www.sziget.hu

A week of massive acts and hundreds of thousands of revellers jammed on to an island in the Danube, it has the mayor in a tizzy over noise levels every year. Don't even think about trying to get there by dinghy. No really, it never works apparently.

ARTS

Carnaval del Pueblo

When: Early August
Where: South London. Parade begins at Elephant and Castle and ends at Burgess Park where the party begins.
Cost: Free
Website: www.carnavaldelpueblo.co.uk

A sea of feathery headdresses, thundering Samba beats and plenty of flesh on show. Oh yes, Europe's largest Latin American event is predictably high-energy, eye-wateringly colourful and hot, hot, hot.

Edinburgh Festival Fringe

When: Most of the month of August
Where: Events held throughout Edinburgh
Cost: Events individually priced
Website: www.edfringe.com

Record-bustlingly enormous – the biggest arts jamboree in the world and the UK's number one tourist attraction – with some 30,000 shows to choose from. Don't play too safe. Stumbling on a gem amongst the dross is a real buzz.

Greenbelt Festival

When: Late August
Where: Cheltenham Racecourse, Cheltenham
Cost: Adult around £80; Concs £52; 13-17 years £43; 4-12 yr olds £39; family ticket £203
Website: www.greenbelt.org.uk

It's a Christian festival so no surprise that Cliff Richard has topped the bill a few times but so have U2, Moby and Billy Bragg. Think tolerance, debate, justice and music rather than happy clapping.

Langholm and Eskdale Music and Arts Festival

When: Mid/Late August
Where: The Buccleuch Centre, Langholm, Scotland
Cost: Events individually priced
Website: www.langholmfestival.co.uk

The site of many a bloody skirmish between Scottish and English raiding parties, nowadays Langholm is a much friendlier place to be. Even the auld enemy is invited to come and enjoy some quality Scottish music and nosh.

National Eisteddfod of Wales

When: Early August
Where: Meirion and District
Cost: £90 for week field ticket
Website: www.eisteddfod.org.uk

Heaven for the Welshophile (if that's actually a word), this is a celebration of Welsh culture, heritage and language that's been going for centuries. It's all in Welsh but English translation is readily available.

Notting Hill Carnival

When: Late August
Where: Notting Hill, London – see website for procession route
Cost: Free
Website: www.nottinghillcarnival.biz

Millions of people, mountains of jerk chicken and much flesh being pressed up against embarrassed policemen. It can only be Notting Hill, now the world's second largest street festival after Rio.

LITERATURE/WRITTEN WORD

Edinburgh International Book Festival

When: Mid/Late August
Where: Charlotte Square Gardens, Edinburgh
Cost: £5-£12 per event per adult, £2-£3.50 per event per child

The Notting Hill Carnival
– a feast for the senses.

Website: www.edbookfest.co.uk
Hundreds of authors and thousands of fanatical book lovers get up close and personal, buff their brain cells, devour books and debate stuff. A civilised oasis amongst the Edinburgh festival mayhem.

FILM

Somerset House Summer Screen
When: Mid August
Where: Safra Fountain Court Open Air cinema, Somerset House
Cost: Events individually priced
Website: www.somersethouse.org.uk/film
Like an incredibly posh drive-in without the cars, enjoy classic and cult movies – Singing in the Rain, Wild at Heart etc – projected on to this famous neoclassical building on the Strand. Proper romantic.

OUTDOORS

Portsmouth International Kite Festival
When: Late August
Where: Southsea Common, Portsmouth
Cost: Free

Website: www.portsmouthkitefestival.org.uk
From the breathtaking to the downright bizarre, lie back and watch an incredible array of soft inflatables drift overhead and stunt kites perform fantastic routines set to music. Do not forget your camera.

ALTERNATIVE ENTERTAINMENT

Egton Bridge Gooseberry Show
When: Mid August
Where: St Hedda's Primary school, Egton Bridge (Nr Whitby). Public admittance from 2pm
Cost: Free
Website: www.egtongooseberryshow.org.uk
Ironic village fetes are fun but this is the real deal. Generations of husbands, wives, friends and neighbours battle it out to grow the heaviest gooseberry.

The Innocent Village Fete
When: Early August
Where: Regent's Park
Cost: Adults £7.50, children £3.50
Website: www.innocentvillagefete.co.uk
Regent's Park goes all villagey for a weekend

Underage? Who cares? – so is everyone else in Victoria Park.

and Londoners embrace their inner yokel by wanging wellies, racing ferrets, showing prize marrows and lolling about in the sun.

FOOD & DRINK

Chilli Fiesta/Totally Tomato Show
When: Early August/Early September
Where: West Dean Gardens, nr Chicester, W. Sussex
Cost: Entry to garden is £7.25 for adults, concessions apply
Website: www.westdean.org.uk/site/gardens/events
A genteel setting with hidden punch, there are over 250 varieties of chilli on show in the Victorian Glasshouse. Or come back in early September and witness amateurs taking on the experts to grow the UK's tastiest tomato.

Great British Beer Festival
When: Early August
Where: Earls Court, London
Tickets: CAMRA member £8, £10 non member. Concessions apply
Website: www.gbbf.org; www.camra.org
Bump bellies, stroke your beard and thrill to the site of this massive exhibition hall dedicated to the great god of beer. There are 450 of the beauties, plus cider, perry and some lagers, so pace yourself.

Pershore Plum Festival
When: Throughout August, cultimates on Plum Day, August Bank Holiday Monday
Where: Throughout Pershore town, Worcestershire
Cost: Free
Website: www.pershoreplumfestival.org.uk
A month-long festival culminates in a whole day of plum crazy goings on – and lots of plummy puns of course – including plum tossing, plum poetry and the chance to eat a lot of plums. Wear purple.

Emma McGowan

septe

'Remember the love' – Anna Jones

illustration Rachel Lattimore

Isle of Wight

www.bestival.net

For most of the year Robin Hill on the Isle of Wight
is an adventure park, which makes it a fitting venue for this most playful of festivals.
Around the fringes, revellers wander in the maze and the nature trail, ride the
toboggan track and clamber through the adventure playground – how often do
you get the opportunity to do those things, especially while drunk, without being
escorted from the premises by stony-faced stewards?

The centrepiece of the three-day festival takes place on Saturday afternoon
when a fancy-dress parade winds noisily through the site, a concept that would
seem to promise rag-week wackiness but plays out more as a surreal carnival (the
2005 event set the world record for the biggest fancy dress party). When, in 2008,
Bestival experienced its first mud bath after four sunny years, you had to salute the
indefatigability of anyone prepared to embrace the somewhat apt underwater
theme and brave the slop dressed as mermaids, Titanic passengers or SpongeBob
SquarePants.

Radio 1's Rob Da Bank and his wife Josie established Bestival in 2004, naming
it after their eccentric independent label Sunday Best. It began as a haven for those
who had come of age with dance culture, but found all-nighters too hectic – 2004's
headliners were Basement Jaxx, Fatboy Slim and Zero 7 – but has expanded its
musical parameters to include fully fledged pop acts (Pet Shop Boys, Scissor Sisters),
adventurous rock bands (Primal Scream, Super Furry Animals) and idiosyncratic

val

Do you take yourself rather
seriously? Then avoid Bestival.

veterans (Billy Bragg, John Martyn). It's worth hanging around for the unannounced special guests: 2008's mystery bookings turned out to be the magnificent Grace Jones and a partially reunited Specials. Meanwhile, the smaller stages, including the dance tents, are getting more impressive every year.

Every festival likes to claim that it's not about the lineup – it's the promoters' traditional insurance against lacklustre headliners – but in Bestival's case it's truer than most. Even with a capacity of just 17,000 (roughly a 10th the size of Glastonbury), it is built for meandering. There are the kind of de rigueur creature comforts that would have been unimaginable during rock festivals' burger-van infancy: a relaxation area called Restival, a creche, even a farmer's market. But beyond them you'll find such novel diversions as the Big Love Inflatable Church (wedding bookings taken) and the solar-powered Groovy Movie Picture House. The festival

page 154 ▶

THE BiGCHiLL recommends

End of the Road
Larmer Tree Gardens, Tollard Royal, near Salisbury, Dorset www.endoftheroadfestival.com

Rather a depressing name for the festival that traditionally winds up the summer season – perhaps they were thinking of 'one for the road'? – but if you can get past that, the End of the Road is a jolly little get-together, a sort of village fete for music fans. Peacocks and parrots roam the beautiful grounds, delighting the genteel audiences; there's a cider bus, an Enchanted Forest and a tent called the Bimble Inn; and if you get bored of the bands, you can gather round the campfire, or join in a game of kubb, a sort of cross between skittles and baseball. With a maximum attendance of 5,000, and a policy of avoiding any sort of corporate sponsorship or advertising, the End of the Road is the ultimate boutique festival.

But what about the music? The organisers, Simon Taffe and Sofia Hagberg, followed their own tastes, which meant a leaning towards low-key, lo-fi Americana (Calexico, Lambchop); folk and its evil twin, anti-folk (Bon Iver, Laura Marling); a bit of raucous garage (the Archie Bronson Outfit); a dash of psychedelia (Mercury Rev). Some have complained that this makes the bill a bit too uniform, too lacking in those unexpected discoveries that can make a festival into something special. But Taffe and Hagberg argue that the surprises are there to be enjoyed; they schedule the weekend so as to let the bands play longer sets, and so 2006 saw I'm From Barcelona climbing the trees to perform from on high.

It seems that the organizers have paid heed as more recent lineups are nothing if not eclectic: the growl of American country legend Steve Earle is countered by the sweet warbling of psych-folk chanteuse Alela Diane. And both are juxtaposed by acts such as Bob Log III, a festival favourite: he's a one-man band who plays slide guitar and drums while wearing full motorcycle leathers and helmet.

There's a Scandinavian touch to the weekend, too, since Hagberg is of Swedish descent. In the Swedish lounge, meatballs are on offer (ah, sweet memories of Ikea!), and there is often a good smattering of Nordic musical treats. What with the balloons, ukuleles, West Country cider, ubiquitous children and even more ubiquitous folkies, the End of the Road is truly the best possible way to say goodbye to the summer.
Carrie O'Grady

also has a daily newspaper, the Bestival Bugle, and 24-hour radio station. All these little details add up. Even ideas that seem a little twee or cosy on paper (a 'sushi yurt'?) become pleasing pit stops on the ground. And if you're pathologically adverse to looking daft, you can relax: the fancy dress is strictly optional.

Being on an island intensifies the sensation that the best festivals generate: the idea that for three days you are sequestered from the real world in a benign community devoted to unquotidian pleasures. While Glastonbury feels like a gathering of disparate tribes, Bestival thrives on a sense of cheerful unity. After one visit, you're likely to want to come back the next year. If even 2008's monsoons couldn't quench Bestival's spirit of puckish adventure, it would seem to be invulnerable.

Dorian Lynskey

Sticking around

The Isle of Wight

If you can't face going home straight after Bestival, you don't have to up tent poles for long. Do yourself a favour and relax on the Isle of Wight for a few extra days and catch what is usually the best weather of the summer.

WHERE TO CAMP

Whether you're camping alone or with kids, Grange Farm Camping and Caravanning Site, Brighstone Bay, is the ideal place to recover from the festival experience. On the opposite half of the island to Bestival the camping ground overlooks the sea and a secluded, fossil-rich beach is a five-minute walk away. And, after you catch up on your sleep, the surrounding rolling countryside is a walker's paradise if exercise takes your fancy.
www.brighstonebay.fsnet.co.uk

For those who travelled without a tent or who are more averse to the elements, Westermill also has several Scandanavian style chalet cottages for rent. Booking essential!
www.westermill.com

WHAT TO DO

Walking

You could challenge yourself by walking the entire 24km of the Tennyson Trail, but that wouldn't leave much time for a pub lunch. The full walk, named, of course, after Alfred Lord Tennyson who moved to the Isle of Wight in 1853, starts just south of Newport and passes Carisbrook Castle, over the Brighstone Downs and through woodland to the Needles – the chalk monolith rocks on the westerly end of the island. A more enjoyable option might be to pick up the walk at Calbourne when there'll only be about 9km between you and a pint of local ale.
www.islandbreaks.co.uk/xsdbimgs/
Tennyson%20Trail.pdf
www.guardian.co.uk/lifeandstyle/2006/
may/20/gowalk.guardianspecial51

The Isle of Wight's famous Needles.

Swimming

The island has 13 Blue Flag beaches – a scheme that promotes sustainable development and promises excellent water quality. In theory, the waves should be at their warmest at this time of year even though the air temperature may not, so full immersion is the best option. For a tranquil swim, head to Colwell Bay on the island's west coast. This small, sandy stretch with nearby amenities is a perfect place to splash about.
www.islandbreaks.co.uk/site/places-to-visit/beach-guide/colwell-bay

Wild spot

With more than 800km of footpaths and bridleways, there couldn't be a more pleasurable way of exploring the island's many nature reserves and diverse wildlife – some of which is rarely glimpsed elsewhere in the British Isles.

Just south-west of Alverstone, at the Alverstone Mead reserve, you can watch birds including the green sandpiper, redshank, kingfisher reed warblers and skylarks. Ancient woodland on the site, managed by Wight Nature Fund, is home to wood sorrel, red currant and wild angelica, and you may catch sight of some of the 12 species of dragonfly or three types of bat. The reserve hosts a thriving community of red squirrels, prevalent on the isle where – unlike the mainland – there are none of their pesky grey cousins.
www.iwight.com/living_here/planning/
Countryside/Nature_Reserves/
Alverstone_Mead/

We dare you

Unsurprisingly, all manner of watersports are catered for on the island. You can easily (or at least, conveniently) learn how to kayak, canoe, surf and windsurf at Wight Water Adventure Watersports centre. And of course, if the Isle of Wight is known round most quarters of the world for a particular aquatic pastime, it's sailing. It's no coincidence that Dame Ellen MacArthur has made her home in Cowes. If you're of the persuasion and bank balance to take a yacht out while on the island, chances are you'll already be in the know, but here's some information for the curious among the rest us.
www.wightwaters.com
www.uksa.org

For skylarks, there's always paragliding. If you have been waiting to take to the skies, best to try it after a little instruction.
www.high-adventure.uk.com

There are few better subjects for a rollicking good ghost yarn than pirates, smugglers and shipwrecks, and as luck would have it, the isle is supposedly the most haunted in the world, if you believe the purveyors of these spooky walks.
www.ghost-tours.co.uk

If it rains

Go back in time at Queen Victoria's Osborne House. Not only impressive in its opulence, the palatial residence offers a rare insight into the intimacy of royal life.
www.english-heritage.org.uk/server/
show/nav.14479

Learn about all things Wight at the Carisbrooke Castle museum, where you

can see artefacts including Victorian clothes, shoes, toys, rifles and lace.
www.carisbrookecastlemuseum.org.uk

FOOD AND DRINK

Beer

Real ale enthusiasts will be in their element with great local brews and pubs to sample them in. Wight-based Goddards Brewery makes several 'Ales of Wight' available throughout the isle during high season. If you're passing, check out the Camra-recommended Folly Inn at Whippingham, near East Cowes. This pub on the river has spectacular views of yachts and dinghies in summer, serves good food and, of course, ales. There is often live entertainment on Thursdays and Saturdays.
www.goddards-brewery.co.uk/
www.wightwash.org.uk/pubpage/
whippingham.html#

Wine

Rosemary vineyard in Ryde is one of the UK's largest wineries and produces award-winning tipples. You can stroll round the vines before getting to work in the tasting rooms.
www.rosemaryvineyard.co.uk

The Romans first planted vines at the Adgestone winery, near Sandown where the current owners are producing award-winning wines. Even the Queen has quaffed the produce from this four-hectare outfit where tours and their 'generous tastings' are popular.
www.adgestonevineyard.co.uk

Local produce

Literally the best bacon on the island is produced by the Isle of Wight Bacon Company, named as a Food Hero by Rick Stein. The company is part of a family farm where pigs are raised in the traditional free-range way 'outside in the sunshine'.
www.isleofwightbacon.co.uk

Newport Farmers' Market (Friday 9–2pm, Saturday 8.30–1pm) is also highly recommended, as is Freshwater on the first Sunday of the month held between 10–2pm.

FOR THE KIDS

If your outdoor wildlife spotting hasn't gone quite to plan, take the kids to Amazon World Zoo where they can see some of the planet's most unusual and endangered creatures and learn about their conservation.
www.amazonworld.co.uk

For all those budding paleontologists in your group, Dinosaur Farm Museum will be an illuminating experience. Their organised fossil hunts are popular with the kids, big and small.
www.isleofwight.com/
dinosaurfarmmuseum/

A baby sloth, just taking it easy at Amazon World Zoo.

septem

Make the most of the month

Curl

As autumn approaches, it's vital to consider new challenges and horizons. Have you contemplated, for example, taking up curling? We thought not, but perhaps it's time to think again. The surprise hit of the 2002 Winter Olympics where we won a gold medal (and winter sports are really not a British thing), this odder-than-odd sport, a kind of bowling on ice, has long been popular in Scotland. Until 2004 there was no dedicated rink south of the border, but all that changed when Fenton's opened in Kent: now you just need to book a session for yourself or for a group, and it's curling stones away.

www.fentonsrink.co.uk

Wallow

Every year the Llanelli Wildfowl & Wetlands Trust tries to remind us that mud, that essential element of wetlands, is glorious. Its mud festival gives us mud hut building, mud facials, mud sculptures and even 'mud food'; more seriously it teaches us about the teeming life of mud flats – the worms, shellfish, wading birds and wildfowl that live within them. In between those huge Welsh skies and the dark Welsh wetlands, you can study the eternal merry-go-round of life.

wwt.org.uk

Belay

Arrr, don't be forgettin' that international Talk Like a Pirate Day is held this month. Avast! Every year various loonies earn thousands for charity by saying 'I be' instead of 'I am' all day. Some of the additions to yer vocabulary might be 'Aye, aye', 'grog' (or you can call it liquor – just don't call it a G&T, my good man, or you'll be keelhauled immediately and if you don't know what keelhauling is, you've got some revision to do), 'me' instead of 'my' (as in 'that's me grog ye've got there, matey') and, of course, a regular 'yo ho ho'. That's the way you laugh when you're a pirate. All right, so mebbe it do be very silly. But it also do be very funny. You can always do with a bit of that.
www.yarr.org.uk

Gobble

September is the month of food festivals in Britain: the two big grandaddies, Abergavenny and Ludlow, go belly to belly within a week of each other. Between the two, you can sample Welsh oggies (pasties to the rest of us), pigeon terrine, tiny Dutch pancakes known as poffertjes, Black Mountain honey, butterscotch crunch ice cream, organic fig relish, Ruddle Court camembert and British truffles all washed down with a glass of fruit wine. It's not just about eating, of course; you can talk about eating too. Foodies such as Tom Parker Bowles, Matt Tebbutt, Mark Hix and Monty Don divide themselves neatly between the two events.
www.abergavennyfoodfestival.com; www.foodfestival.co.uk

203

Plunge

This is the time, after the long hot months of July and August (we hope) for outdoor swimming. You need a good picnic, a picturesque spot by the sea or a lake (there's a lovely beach at Loch Lomond if you're not frightened of the cold), a dry towel and a little bit of sunshine. The secret is to strip off and jump straight in, then swim as fast as possible away from the shore, removing the temptation to get straight out again. After a minute or two the shock wears off, then your body tingles all over and does not stop tingling for a good half hour. It is delicious.

www.outdoorswimmingsociety.co.uk

Grind

How can anyone resist an event billing itself as 'the world's leading award show for Elvis tribute artists'? The south Wales town of Porthcawl is the unlikely destination for all these pilgrims, who gather once a year to compare their In the Ghettos and their Suspicious Minds. Of course, the chance that these impersonators have the looks, snake hips and filthily sexual energy of the young Elvis is fairly small. But they come to pay tribute to youth and beauty, and to the sadness of middle age, with beautiful music and the odd pelvic thrust. Really, what more could you want? Cheeseburgers? They're also available.

www.elvies.co.uk

Nose around

To make the most of an Open House visit, you have to overcome one issue: how do you make it look as if you're there in the spirit of architectural curiosity and community-mindedness when you nakedly just want to poke round someone else's home? The trick is to simply remember ... they asked for it! No one would put their home on the Open Houses list if they weren't quietly thrilled at the idea of people wandering around and murmuring to each other, 'Can you believe they've got matching Eames chairs?' With that in mind, get poking.

www.heritageopendays.org.uk; www.londonopenhouse.org

Shimmy

The word mela is Sanskrit for gathering, and every year all across the Indian subcontinent villages, towns and cities hold their melas, just as Spanish towns hold their ferias. Now the habit is taking hold in the UK: the Newcastle Mela is one of the largest in the north-east and is organised by the Punjabi, Pakistani, Bengali and Hindu populations in the area. As you'd expect, the food is always fantastic, and there's dancing, music, funfairs and face-painting everywhere you look.
www.newcastle.gov.uk/core.nsf/a/mela_home

Spook

As the nights get longer and the evenings darker, you might like to spook yourself with the famous Ghost Hunt of York. This tour has been meandering through the streets of 'the most haunted city in the world' for years now: its leaders boast that they never miss a night and the guest book on their website is packed with rave reviews. Using jokes, tricks and a few (apparently accurate) stories, they bring the long history of the streets of York to life.
www.ghosthunt.co.uk

Bibi van der Zee

Summer

Navigating without a map

So you're out for a walk in the hills when, still some miles from your destination, the battery in your GPS gives up the ghost. Undismayed, you dig around in your bag for the map and compass. The map and compass you left on the table in the morning. There's no one around you can ask for directions and there are no convenient signposts. Oops.

Fortunately, all is not lost. Assuming you have a rough idea of the direction you should be taking – be it north, east, south or west – there are many different ways of orientating yourself so that you can continue your journey with some degree of confidence.

Using the sun

We all know that the sun rises in the east and sets in the west (although somewhat imprecisely). Helpfully, at its highest point – around the middle of the day – it also points due south. If you find yourself in the southern hemisphere, the sun will be due north at its zenith.

At any other time of day, set your watch to the true local time (so if it's British Summer Time, for instance, put your watch back an hour) then, holding it horizontally, point the hour hand at the sun. The line that bisects the angle between the hour hand and the 12 on your watch will point south. In the southern hemisphere, point the 12 towards the sun. The line that bisects the angle between the 12 and the hour hand will point north.

iving

Using the stars

If you happen to be out at night and the sky is clear, finding the pole star, which will give you a pretty good north bearing, is a relatively simple affair. First, look for Ursa Major, the constellation popularly known as the Plough or the Big Dipper (though its seven stars more accurately resemble a long-handled saucepan). The two stars that interest us are the ones that form the side of the saucepan away from the handle. These two point upwards towards the top star in the constellation Cassiopeia, instantly recognisable as a big bright W. About half way along this imaginary line between Ursa Major and Cassiopeia you will notice a bright star. That's Polaris, the northern pole star.

In the southern hemisphere, you'll need your wits about you. First, find two very bright stars on the horizon – Alpha and Beta Centauri, the Pointer Stars. Draw an imaginary line between these two and at the midpoint take a line out at 90 degrees towards a third very bright star, Achernar, a long way over to the right. Now, the Pointer Stars are so called because they point up to the Southern Cross, a five-star constellation. Draw a line from left to right through the horizontal axis of this cross and keep going, and the point where it hits your first line will be more or less over the South Pole. Nobody said it was easy.

Alternatively, seek help from Orion (see page 29), which can be seen from both hemispheres. This is a constellation that rises and sets, so if the night is yet young it will be due east. At the end of the night it will be lying due west.

Using a pin

Another trick that works in both hemispheres. If you have a sewing kit and a bit of silk on you, take a needle and tie a piece of thread round it roughly half way down (so that the needle is horizontal when hanging by the thread). Rub the needle repeatedly on the silk, always in the same direction, from the eye towards the head. Now take the thread, dangle the needle and the head will point north. Obviously, if you have a magnet to use in place of the silk, this will work even better. If you do not have any thread, float the needle in still water on a small scrap of paper or a blade of grass.

Using a stick

Pop a stick at least a metre long into the ground, making it as upright as you can. Place a small stone on the spot where the stick's shadow ends. Wait for at least 15 minutes then place a new stone where the tip of the shadow has moved. Draw a line between the two stones – the first stone will point west, the second one east (and vice versa in the southern hemisphere). Draw another line at right angles to this for north and south.

Using water

Finally, if you find yourself irredeemably lost and you come to a watercourse of any sort, follow it downstream: waterways almost inevitably lead to centres of population. Once you have found a house with someone in it, you can swallow your pride and ask where on earth it is you are. They might even lend you a map.

Dixe Wills

Summer

Birdwatching

There are two difficulties when it comes to identifying birds. The first is that, all too frequently, they flit by too quickly to get a good look at them. The second is that, when they do stay in the same place for a decent amount of time, they look a bit too much like some other bird for a positive ID to be made with any conviction. Thankfully, there are two ways to get your own back. You can commit to memory a few easy rules for distinguishing between birds that look alike; perhaps even better, learn what they sound like so you can start to name birds without even seeing them. Imagine how your friends will gasp in awe.

By sight

Great tits and blue tits

By adapting from a life in the woods to a life among humans – and their bird tables – these two have transformed themselves into the commonest garden birds in many parts of Britain. The great tit is **great** on account of it being one of the larger members of the tit family. The blue tit is so called because the top of its head is a lovely pastel **blue** (the great tit's head is black). If you can't see the tops of their heads, look at their breasts – the great tit has a thick black line running down the centre.

Swifts and swallows

If a bird goes swooping around you in summer like a paper aeroplane, the chances are it is a swallow or a swift (if you see what you think is a really tiny swallow, it's probably a martin). They both spend their winters in sub-Saharan Africa and make the long and dangerous journey each year to summer in Europe. Telling them apart is simpler than you might imagine. Swallows spend much of their time congregating on telephone wires, where you can look out for their distinctive red

chilling

chins. Swifts, however, have tiny feet on which all four toes point forward, making wire-sitting an impossibility. If still in doubt, remember that, in flight, the swift is dark brown underneath but the swallow has milky-white underparts (and milk is something nice to **swallow**).

(Clockwise from top): blue tit, great tit, swallow and swift.

(Clockwise from top): rook, carrion crow, common gull, herring gull and black-headed gull.

Rooks and carrion crows

There's an old saying: 'If you see one rook, it's a crow: if you see lots of crows, they're rooks.' Although this does not always hold true, it must be said that rooks are sociable types while crows prefer a more solitary existence. This is why we can speak of the existence of rookeries but not croweries. The definitive test is to look at the bill: while the carrion crow has black feathers underneath, the rook has a bare patch of skin there, which makes it look as though it's wearing a balaclava.

Confusingly, the wider crow family (corvidae) includes rooks, jackdaws, ravens and others as well as crows. Therefore, if all else fails, you can call any one of them a crow and still be technically correct.

Gulls

Britain's three commonest gulls are the black-headed gull, the herring gull and the common gull. Just to confuse things, the head of the black-headed gull is actually brown in summer and white with a dark spot on each side in winter. Herring gulls do eat herring among a vast range of other things, which is, perhaps, what makes them so enormous. This is the gull whose 'key-owk, key-owk' call is the one we associate with the seaside. They have grey wings, tipped with black, and their white heads become streaked with grey in winter. The common gull, meanwhile, is not all that common in Britain any more and you're most likely to spot it in winter. Similar in colouration to the herring gull, the common gull is much smaller and with greenish rather than pink legs.

By sound

Blackbird

If there's a cat on the prowl you'll hear the blackbird's urgent alarm call – a continuous shrill 'pink-pink-pink-pink-pink' a bit like a smoke alarm.

Rooks and carrion crows

Can't get a good look at their bills? Then listen out for the raucous and unmistakable 'korr' of the crow. The rook makes a distinctly different 'karr' sound.

Woodpigeon

Wander into any wood anywhere in Britain and sooner or later you'll hear a loud rhythmic but slightly hoarse 'wa-waaaah-wah wa-wah' soaring over the treetops.

Tawny owl

'To-wit woo-hoo' is possibly the most famous bird cry in Britain but it's too often ascribed to the barn owl (which instead utters a shriek, when it says anything at all). Only the male tawny can sing both parts of the song – the female can only manage the 'to-wit'.

Dixe Wills

Fooling a

Outdoor romps

As the song goes, mad dogs and Englishmen go out in the noonday sun – and, on the rare occasions when it appears, that same sun can turn ordinary, reticent Brits into mad dogs themselves, shagging wherever and whenever they please. All across this green and pleasant land, people are getting down to it in the open – more than you'd think. Last year, the Scotsman surveyed 1,0000 of its readers and found nearly 40 per cent had had sex outside. They're a patriotic bunch: one of the top places in the UK for dogging, or exhibitionistic outdoor sex that is watched by voyeurs, is on the site of the Battle of Culloden, near Nairn. Scotland the Brave, indeed.

Historic battlegrounds aside, though, the number one spot to cosy up is the beach. Pebbled ones are not recommended, for obvious reasons, which knocks out most of Kent. But sandy stretches backed by sheltered dunes are more popular, especially Studland Bay in Dorset, which is thronged with frisky couples in heat-waves. (One year the police decided to crack down on bad behaviour there – much to the delight of the miscreants, since it was an undercover operation and the cops all had to strip off.)

Summer also provides a perfect opportunity for the British male to unite his two great passions: sport and shagging. A couple of years ago, Ascot had to call in the Old Bill after security found teenagers had broken through the fence and on to the racetrack to drink and have sex. The Sun newspaper reports that a couple had sex in the stands during a test match at Trent Bridge, Nottingham. And, rather sweetly, a boy and a girl were kicked out of Rugby school for fooling around on the pitch – the very birthplace of rugby.

But it's at festivals where people really try it on, though not always with the desired result. Problems are legion, even for well-established couples. Picture this: it's late, it's dark, and you've rounded off a wonderful day by having umpteen ciders with your loved one. Now you're all cosy in the tent, with your sleeping bags zipped together and your muddy feet happily entwined. All around is quiet. What's to stop you having a sneaky shag? Nothing – except for the fact that there

are probably 30 people within a 20ft radius, separated from you by nothing more than a few layers of nylon that's about as soundproof as clingfilm, and who will hear not only your moans of ecstasy but also every little slurp, squelch and rasp that accompanies your joyous coupling. There's a way to strike back, though: in the morning, be sure to remark loudly and often that you wished those horny bastards had kept the bloody noise down, 'cause you didn't get a wink of sleep.

Then there's the hygiene issue. 'After a couple of days, I don't even want to sleep with myself, let alone someone else,' says one punter. Thank God, then, for the 'ladywash' team: a few blokes who have been seen at festivals next to a small paddling pool full of water, along with some soap and sponges, offering to wash the intimate parts of any females who might feel the need. How thoughtful!

Done right, though, in a quiet, deserted spot, al fresco sex can be one of the great joys of the British summer, allowing one to commune with nature in a subversive, Wicker Man sort of way. It can even encompass more innocent pleasures. One woman recalls going so far in her search for a secluded woodland spot that she disturbed a snoozing owl. 'I don't know what variety it was, but it was huge – we heard this massive flapping of wings. I'd never seen one before, and probably never will again. It was beautiful.' Bet you don't get that in the car park for the monument to the Battle of Culloden.

Top tips

● Don't try this in Dubai. Unless you really like foreign jails.

● Don't get caught. Outdoor sex is not illegal, so long as there is 'a reasonable expectation of privacy'. But if someone sees you and isn't happy about it, you could be charged with outraging public decency.

● Don't get filmed. That YouTube link will go around your office like wildfire.

● Do go swimming in the sea. Blokes may think the cold water will have an adverse effect, but give it 15 minutes after you get out and your circulation will be zinging – with happy results.

● Do come prepared with mosquito repellent, sunscreen, towel, easily removed undergarments and, if applicable, extra condoms – in case you drop the first one.

● Do shut up. No one wants to hear you sounding like a bad porn film. Really.

● Do watch out for nettles. And gorse. And, more importantly, the tide.

● Don't sneak into the bushes at festivals. People pee there – and worse.

● Don't think of Robin Askwith, Barbara Windsor or any other B-grade 1960s smutcom, as you will surely collapse into giggles and start doing your Sid James imitation laugh.

Carrie O'Grady

Festival People

Jerry Morgan
the Groovy Movie Picture House

Before I started touring festivals with my solar-powered cinema in 1997, I'd been on the free festival circuit for a while. I had an interest in film and a lot of film-makers I knew had trouble finding somewhere to get their work seen. Festivals seemed to include all sorts of art forms apart from film. Through the free festival circuit and living on the road I'd got experience of making things, so I thought, why not a cinema?

The first time around it was pretty makeshift: we hung a sheet off the side of a lorry and projected the film on to that. Then I got a saggy old army tent and for a while we were using a generator – but that made loads of noise and besides I wanted, if I could, to use renewable energy. That was the way we lived. So we bought a couple of photovoltaic panels for the next show. Then I got a Lottery grant and used it to buy a custom-built marquee and reliable equipment. Events started to take us seriously and, over the years, the money earned was used to develop the project into a high-quality multimedia venue.

We do Glastonbury every year and we used to do the Big Green Gathering. I usually get to Wychwood, Stokes Bay and Bestival, and we love going to a great festival in Holland called Ruigoord Landjuweel held in a small village that has been squatted for 30 years. My own favourite festivals are Shambala, which has been running for 18 years in Northamptonshire, and Lounge on the Farm, held at Merton Farm in Kent, usually has a really good lineup: they're quite small, full of character and far less commercial than most.

We show a wide range of independent films about all sorts of subjects such as environmental issues and activism. These have included Garbage Warrior about a man who makes extraordinary carbon-neutral houses, and On the Verge, a film about anti-arms campaigners that the police tried to shut down when it came out. Now that the internet has really come of age, it's got so much easier for these films to be seen, but there's noth-

ing quite like seeing it on a proper screen. There's a community feel to watching it together that you just can't get from staring at your computer screen.

The festival circuit has definitely changed a lot – it all seems quite posh now. It always amazes me when people come along and spend £1,000 on some plush accommodation. But on the plus side, the food has improved massively. When I started all you could ever get was a 40p egg butty and a 30p cup of tea. Now you can get food from every corner of the world, all beautifully prepared.

I'm 42, and you'd think after all these years I'd get tired of it, but it's still a lot of fun. The thing I like about festivals is the way that people forget what they should be doing, forget their daily lives, and just let their guard down. They let themselves be silly, chat to people they wouldn't normally chat to, do things they'd not normally contemplate. Festivals are an amazing mixing pot of people, and that's one thing that's really changed for the better – you get a much wider range of people coming now.

My favourite thing is late at night – the cinema is usually allowed to run after the music stages have had to shut down – when people wandering past just get drawn in and find themselves getting involved in one of our multimedia performances. The shows involve film, an accordion and ukulele, some songs and video remixing. You never know quite what's going to happen, and that's what I like – those moments when it all goes a bit sideways.

www.groovymovie.biz

Dish of the

Levi's lip-smackin' stew

From Big Chill regular Levi Roots

Levi ROOTS

Serves 3–4

For the filling:
- 1 jar of Jamaican Brown Stew Cooking Sauce
- 3 chicken breasts, sliced thickly
- ½ green pepper, cut into small dice
- ½ carrot, peeled and cut into strips
- A sprig of thyme
- A sprig of mint
- 2 tbsp vegetable oil
- Salt & pepper to season

month

Method:

- Heat the oil in a pan until hot, then add the chicken strips and fry until cooked through and golden brown.

- Take the chicken out of the pan and place on kitchen paper to drain any excess oil.

- Heat a jar of Jamaican Brown Stew Sauce in a separate saucepan, then add the peppers, carrots and herbs.

- Bring to the boil, then leave to simmer slowly for 5 minutes.

- Stir in the cooked chicken and serve with rice or vegetables. Enjoy!

Drink of th

Hot bramble
From the Big Chill bartenders

Gently **simmer** (do not boil) for 20 minutes and **serve** piping hot.

Makes 12 drinks

Bottle merlot red wine
350ml Southern Comfort
500ml clear apple juice
Strawberry puree
Raspberry puree
100g caster sugar
3 sticks cinnamon or 2 tsp
   ground cinnamon
Six large dashes
   Angostura bitters

e month

Game of

Grand day out bingo

Part treasure hunt, part bingo, this game is an excellent way to make the most of your grand day out. And you'll get a cracking set of photographs to make it even more memorable.

Make a list of all the things that you think you could see or do on your outing: get everyone involved and be as ridiculous, fantastical, creative and outrageous as possible, because there is every chance that you'll find all manner of weird and wonderful things lurking in the most unlikely places. What kind of people will you see? What might you find under that bridge? You could start gathering ideas before you arrive, a guaranteed way to generate excitement.

Make up as many bingo cards as there are people. Each card could have 10, 20 or 30 squares on, each with something from your list in it – how many depends on how good a hunter you think you are. If the weather report looks bad, drop each card in a plastic wallet before you set off, and make sure there are enough pens and digital cameras (or camera phones) and spare batteries to go around.

Dedicate a few hours or the whole day to the bingo game – the beauty of this one is that you can play it while you take part in all the other activities you want to do. Just keep an eye out for the things on your card, take a photograph every time you spot something, and mark it off. The sillier and more memorable the picture, the better your photo album will be when you get home. First to mark off a line on their card gets a small prize, as does the first to mark off two. Get a full house and you are the day's winner.

Perri Lewis

September festival directory

MUSIC

BIG ONES

Bestival
When: Early September
Where: Robin Hill Country Park, Isle of Wight
Cost: Adult weekend including camping is £140
Website: www.bestival.net
Ever wondered what a radio DJ's dream festival would look like? This is it. Boutique camping, a Bollywood cocktail bar, hidden discos, inflatable church weddings, pay-per-poo loos and a massive line up of big and breaking names.

End of the Road
When: Mid September
Where: Larmer Tree Gardens, Wiltshire
Cost: Adult weekend including camping is £115
Website: www.endoftheroadfestival.com
Back to basics festival with a 5,000 capacity that prides itself on no branding and sponsorhip, and no over-hyped bands on the bill. The organisers sold their house to get it going. So far, so good.

ROCK/INDIE

Alchemy Festival
When: Mid September
Where: A secret location in Lincolnshire
Cost: Adult tickets around £50, Teen £22, Child £8. Parking and camping extra
Website: www.alchemyfestival.co.uk
Conjuring up a bit of small festival magic in a secret location with promises of giant fire bubbles, glow in the dark treasure hunts, fresh eggs of a morning and live music.

Jersey Live
When: Early September
Where: Jersey, Channel Islands
Cost: Around £80 for a weekend ticket
Website: www.jerseylive.org.uk
The island famous for cows and Bergerac now has a decent mid-sized festival to boast about. Going since 2004, line-ups have included the Zutons, Basement Jaxx and the Prodigy.

Loopallu
When: Mid September
Where: Ullapool, Ross and Cromarty, Scotland
Cost: £55; camping £15 extra; campervans/caravans £25; Under-12s FREE
Website: www.loopallu.co.uk
The far north west of Scotland is rapidly becoming the place to finish off the summer. An intimately sized festival with a friendly crowd, the likes of Franz Ferdinand on the bill and fringe events in the local boozers.

DANCE/ELECTRONICA

Newfoundland Secret Summer Gathering
When: Early September
Where: Secret location, probably in mid-Wales
Cost: around £30
Website: www.newfoundlandfestival.org.uk
Somewhere in Wales (probably) a bunch of guerilla contemporary artists and electronic music fanatics are creating a woodland

wonderland of dance, poetry and handmade decor. Full on visuals and big sounds.

Waveform

When: Mid September
Where: Liddington, near Swindon, Wiltshire
Cost: Around £90 for 3 days including camping, child £22
Website: www.waveformfestival.com
Stand – or rather, dance – together for peace with likeminded ravers round the world. Part of the Global Dance Festival for Peace offering the best underground dance music, big lightshows and lots of peaceful thoughts, man.

FOLK

BunkFest

When: Early September
Where: Wallingford, Oxfordshire
Cost: around £10
Website: www.bunkfest.co.uk
What started out as a local publican's 50th birthday party has grown into an annual celebration of music, dance, steam and beer. Named after a local branch line, don't miss the singing steam train.

Folkfest

When: Early September
Where: venues around Burnham-on-Sea, Somerset
Cost: FREE
Website: www.folkfest.co.uk
Acoustic gigs all weekend in pubs around town, a street market, open mic sessions, tons of stuff for kids and an outdoor concert on the Sunday. And all of it free.

Fylde Folk Festival

When: Early September
Where: Marine Hall, Fleetwood, Fylde, Lancashire
Cost: Weekend tickets £55
Website: www.fylde-folk-festival.com
A quality line up of folk festival favourites with a special helping of extras like clog dancing contests, a competition to find the

worst singer in the world and late night ceilidhs.

Off The Tracks Late Festival

When: Early September
Where: Donington Park Farmhouse, Isley Walton, nr Castle Donington, Leicestershire
Cost: £60 for weekend including camping; children (12-16) £27.50
Website: www.offthetracks.co.uk
Get thoroughly put back together after a long summer with a spot of chanting and meditation and some roots, folk and dance music. The spirit of Glastonbury is alive and well in Leicestershire.

CLASSICAL/JAZZ

Scarborough Jazz Festival

When: Late September
Where: Scarborough Spa building, Scarborough
Cost: Around £50 weekend, Around £30 day
Website: www.scarboroughjazzfestival.co.uk
Mostly British musicians with a few international names thrown into the mix, expect the likes of Courtney Pine and the BBC Big Band performing jazz standards in the UK's original seaside resort.

INTERNATIONAL

Lake of Stars Festival

When: End September/Early October
Where: Senga Bay, Malawi
Cost: £40 for 3 days and nights
Website: www.lakeofstars.org
Be the envy of your stuck-in-the-mud mates by going to a festival where you'll need your sunnies rather than your wellies. Global stars and sensational local talent on the shores of a shimmering African lake.

Get yourself to Malawi and
celebrate life at the Lake of Stars.

ARTS

The London Gathering
When: Throughout September
Where: Events through London
Cost: See website
Website: www.thelondongathering.com
Get your kilt on and gather the clans. Famous and non-famous Scots, and presumably a few English, gather in praise of the best Scottish food, music, arts, fashion etc in London.

Molten Festival
When: Late September through to October
Where: Various venues in Barking and Dagenham, Greater London
Cost: £17/£15 or £45 for a Month of Sundays pass
Website: www.barking-dagenham.gov.uk/4-arts-culture/molten/molten-main.html
Six years old and now Barking and Dagenham's flagship event for the Cultural Olympiad, this is five weeks of concerts, variety shows, street theatre and tie-ins with local schools.

Rye Festival
When: Mid/Late September
Where: Rye, Surrey
Cost: See website
Website: www.ryefestival.co.uk
Mainly classical music with a heavyweight fringe (debates about journalism and global warming etc). Lighter touches from the likes of Paul Merton introducing silent movies and Michael Rosen doing party poetry, part stand up for kids.

Tenby Arts Festival
When: Mid/End September
Where: Throughout Tenby
Cost: Various some free
Website: www.tenbyartsfest.co.uk
Local Welsh multi-arts festival beside miles of wide sandy beaches, there's fully staged opera, massed male voice choirs and international music alongside sand sculpture competitions and fringe frolics on the beach.

Thames Festival
When: Mid September
Where: London
Cost: Free
Website: www.thamesfestival.org
Bringing normal London life to a standstill for two days between Westminster and Tower Bridges with a street carnival, a parkour/free run zone, fireworks and river races.

LITERATURE/WRITTEN WORD

Aspects – A celebration of Irish Writing
When: Late September
Where: North Down Heritage Centre, Town Hall, Bangor, County Down
Cost: Various/free
Website: www.northdown.gov.uk
Everything you'd expect from a leading litfest – erudite chat, razor sharp politics, poetic outpourings and the cream of Irish talent. Expect big hitters like Seamus Heaney and Marian Keyes alongside up and coming talent.

Bath Festival of Children's Literature
When: Late September
Where: Bath
Cost: Various
Website: www.bathkidslitfest.co.uk
Guest lists from previous years read like a who's-who of the children's book scene – Shirley Hughes, Michael Rosen, Nick Butterworth etc – there are imaginative events for babies upwards.

Bristol Poetry Festival
When: Early/Mid September
Where: Bristol Old Vic and other venues in the city
Cost: Events free or individually priced
Website: www.poetrycan.co.uk
Always the bridesmaid, never the bride. Well, not here it's not. Poetry gets to fling the bouquet with two weeks of poetry slams and surgeries, recitals, open mic sessions and famous names.

Havant Literary Festival
When: End September
Where: Havant, Hants
Cost: Events individually priced
Website: www.havantlitfest.hampshire.org.uk
Good, solid festival on the south coast showcasing local talent and serving up tasty talks by authors like Fay Weldon, Murray Lachlan Young and Ronald Harwood.

Henley Literary Festival
When: Mid/Late September
Whre: Henley on Thames
Cost: Events individually priced
Website: www.henleyliteraryfestival.co.uk
Like a handsome public schoolboy, this one is only young but it already has more confidence and class than average. River readings, historic venues and the likes of Michael Palin, India Knight, Kate Adie and Irvine Welsh.

Islay Book Festival
When: Early September
Where: Port Ellen Primary School, Isle of Islay, Scotland
Cost: See website
Website: www.islaybookfestival.co.uk
What? A book group that actually reads rather than just sinking bottles of wine? This lot won a prize for the quality of their bookish chat and started a festival. Swots. A few years on and they're pulling in the likes of Iain Banks.

Litcamp
When: Mid September
Where: Tower Building, London Metropolitan University
Cost: £36 including entry to all sessions, lunch, morning and afternoon coffee.
Website: www.litcamp.org
Writers emerge blinking from their garrets and bunkers to spend a whole glorious day mingling with agents, publishers and other writers. Bend ears, pick brains and network like crazy, then retreat to safety again.

Small Wonder
When: Mid September
Where: Charleston, East Sussex
Cost: Saturday all day £27, workshops £135, all event ticket £95
Website: www.charleston.org.uk/smallwonder
Dedicated to the delicate art of the short story but not short on big names the likes of Anne Enright, Gerald Scarfe, Zadie Smith and Lionel Shriver. There's also a popular short story slam for wannabes.

West London Literary Festival
When: Early September
Where: Acton Green
Costs: Various/free
Website: www.ealing.gov.uk
Small but satisfying newbie on the circuit offering the usual festive fare of author talks – Andrew Motion, Richard Briers, Melissa Benn etc – workshops, storytelling sessions and recitals.

York Book Fair
When: Mid September
Where: Knavesmire Suite, York Racecourse, York
Cost: Free
Website: www.yorkbookfair.com
Breathe in the fug of over 100,000 rare, antiquarian and out of print books at Europe's biggest book fair but beware. You could end up losing hours of your life and spending tens of thousands of pounds.

OUTDOORS

Braemar Gathering
When: First Saturday in September
Where: The Princess Royal and Duke of Fife Memorial Park, Braemar, Scotland
Cost: Tickets from £14-£17 depending on stand
Website: www.braemargathering.org
Yes, this is the real deal – blokes who look like the Scots porridge oats man flinging tree trunks into the air. Ancient Highland sports

plus traditional dancing and piping, often presided over by the Queen.

The Great River Race
When: Early September
Where: Race begins at Islands Gardens opposite Greenwich and ends at Ham Street Riverside.
Cost: Spectating is free, for entry details check website
Website: www.greatriverrace.co.uk
Pish and tish to boat races with only two teams. Let's have 300 motley vessels, arcane rules about numbers of oars and a London Marathon-esque mixture of fun racers and those who are deadly serious about winning.

Isle of Wight Cycling Festival
When: Mid/Late September
Where: All over the Isle of Wight
Cost: See website
Website: www.sunseaandcycling.com
Join 4,500 or so other big-thighed cycling devotees to explore trails all over the island. If you relish a challenge, pedal yourself across the river in the 'Sink or Swim' or enter the 'Hills Killer', which is presumably quite steep.

White Air Extreme Sports Festival
When: Mid September
Where: Brighton Beach, Brighton
Cost: Around £20, children under 7 go free
Website: www.whiteair.co.uk
Think of every crazy white-knuckle thing you can do in the air or the sea and it will probably be on display here and available to try (go on, go on). The less daredevil can check out the beach volleyball.

ALTERNATIVE

National Mud Festival of Wales
When: Early September
Where: National Wetland Centre, Llanelli
Cost: Free to WWT members, entry for others is £7.30 adult, Child 4-16 £4.
Website: www.wwt.org.uk
Oh the irony. If you haven't had enough mud, mud, glorious festival mud for one summer try your hand at making mud pies, enter the mud-of-war or just enjoy the wildlife on the estuary mudflats.

Drink up your cider! It's FolkFest in Somerset.

Take a break from the Highland Feast by the shores of Loch Lomond.

Porthcawl Elvis Festival

When: Late September
Where: Porthcawl, N Wales
Cost: Events are at various prices from £5 to £30
Website: www.elvies.co.uk
Vegas comes to North Wales as hundreds of Elvises battle it out to win Best Welsh Elvis, Best Gospel Elvis and the coveted Gold Lame Jacket. Breakfast at the Heartbreak Hotel is a sight not to be missed. Uh huh huh.

FOOD AND DRINK

Abergavenny Food Festival

When: Mid September
Where: Abergavenny town centre
Cost: Events individually priced
Website: www.abergavennyfoodfestival.com
Lush food served up in the gateway to the Brecon Beacons National Park. Expect demos, celeb chefs, market stalls galore, hog roasts, fishing expeditions and lots of gluttons thoroughly enjoying themselves.

Aldeburgh Food and Drink Festival

When: Late September
Where: Snape Maltings, Nr Aldeburgh, Suffolk
Cost: Events individually priced
Website: www.aldeburghfoodanddrink.co.uk
The archetypal foodie's paradise showcasing over seventy local artisan producers and featuring talks and demos from Michelin starred chefs like Tom Aikens and Galton Blackiston.

Brighton and Hove Food and Drink Festival

Where: Brighton, various locations
When: Throughout September
Cost: Events individually priced
Website: www.brightonfoodfestival.co.uk
Slurp, suck, nibble, lick and bust a gut in the UK's hippest city by the sea. The focus is on sampling quality regional produce, debating food issues and supporting local restaurants and artisans.

Fishstock Brixham

When: Mid September
Where: Seafood Pavillion, Fish Quay, Brixham, Devon
Cost: around £7
Website: www.fishstockbrixham.co.uk
A somewhat offbeat combo of fish and music, all in the name of a good cause. Fishy

daytime activities give way to nighttime music with proceeds going to help the UK's beleaguered fishing communities.

Great British Cheese Festival
When: Late September
Where: Cheltenham
Cost: Events individually priced
Website: www.thecheeseweb.com
As Wimbledon is to tennis, so this festival is to cheese. The bee's knees of cheese, you could say. Obviously, loads of cheese to eat and buy, plus cheese masterclasses, cheese tossing, cheese skittles. You get the idea.

Highland Feast
When: Late September
Where: Locations throughout the Highlands, see website for event details
Cost: Events individually priced
Website: www.highlandfeast.co.uk
Eat, drink and generally overdo it at tastings, mushroom forages, high teas on the golf course, bramble picking rambles, distillery tours and gourmet dinners. Try to lift your head out of the trough long enough to notice the stunning Highland setting.

Ludlow Food and Drink Festival
When: Mid September
Where: Ludlow town centre
Cost: Ranges from £5.50 to £6.50 for adults and £13-£15 for families.
Website: www.foodfestival.co.uk
In a town whose food is far from ordinary – three Michelin-starred and eight AA-rosetted restaurants if you please – comes a food festival with similarly sparkling credentials. Bang goes the diet again.

Mold Food and Drink Festival
When: Mid September
Whre: Mold, North East Wales
Cost: Events individually priced
Website: www.moldfoodfestival.co.uk
If food really is the new rock and roll then festivals like this must be the pudding of proof. Celebrity chefs cook up a storm in the cookery theatre and even the young folk join in with a teen cuisine competition.

Nantwich Food and Drink Festival
When: Late September
Where: Nantwich town centre, Cheshire
Cost: Free entry, possible charge for some events
Website: www.nantwichfoodfestival.co.uk
Let your belt out a couple of notches, there's more to Cheshire than just cheese. Get stuck in to local treats like regional beers, spices, chocolate, fruit wines, ice cream, cup cakes and, okay, a fair bit of cheese.

Organic Food Festival
When: Early September
Where: Bristol, Corn Street area
Cost: Events individually priced, much free
Website: www.soilassociation.org/festival
One hundred percent pesticide-free fun in the UK's self-proclaimed green capital. All the usual foodie fare – demos, tastings, talks etc – but with an extra soupcon of worthiness and probably the tastier for it.

York Festival of Food and Drink
When: Mid/Late September
Where: York, various locations
Cost: Events individually priced
Website: www.yorkfoodfestival.com
Serious food fest that draws in 150,000 visitors every day. Events are loosely hooked round a theme each time – past ones have included 'learn' and 'crude food' (stop sniggering, it means raw or simple food not funny shaped veg).

Emma McGowan

233

INDEX

Acknowledgements

Big Chill would like to thank:

The team at HQ:
Ali Khan, Alice Sharp, Caro Russell, Caroline Babington, Chris Greenwood, Clint Welsh, Dan Heath, Etienne Pansegrauw, Eugenie Arrowsmith, Guy Morley, Katrina Larkin, Kelly Landau, Mark Fuller (Sparky), Monica Wolff, Nigel Foster, Paul Ryan, Richard Bigg, Serhiy Horobets, Shep, Stu Archer, Suzi Green, Tom Sweet, Victoria Burns

The Big Chill Bar Crew:
Aoife Halliday, Grace West, Karin Romarker, Lina Stanionyte, Rory Martin, Sandra Arvidsson and the team at The Big Chill House and Bar.

And also:
Alex Lee Thomson and Karen Johnson at Orbit Pr, Annie Nightingale, Carmel Mulhall at 360 Communications, Claire Nightingale at PBJ Management, Clothilde Redfern and Peter Carlton at Film4, Dan De Sausmarez at Dusted, David Puzey and Matthew Darcy Hunt at Bleach, Hector Proud, Kate Statham and Zoe Stainsby at Idea Generation, Levi Roots, Lisa Woodman and Lucy Granville at The Big Issue, Lol Hammond, Matt Black, Mr Scruff, Murray Clark, Norman Jay MBE, Paul Hartnoll, Phill Hartnoll, Pete Lawrence, Robert Altman, Stuart Semple and Tom Middleton.

Guardian Books would like to thank:

Phil Daoust, Cameron Fitch, Perri Lerris, Dorian Lynskey, Emma McGowan, Charlotte Northedge, Carrie O'Grady, Alexis Petridis, Jude Rogers, Dee Rudebeck, Dixe Wills, Bibi van der Zee.

Illustration acknowledgements

2-3: Steve Razzetti; 4-5: Kelvin Webb; 6: Andrew Carthy; 9: Sophie Laslett; 10-11 (photo): Sergey Chushkin/shutterstock, (illustration): Ryan Miglinczy; 13 (main): Edd Westmacott/shot2bits.net, (inset): Anni Timms; 14 (main): Edd Westmacott/shot2bits.net, (inset): Maria Jefferis/shot2bits.net; 15 (main): shutterstock, (inset): Mike Burnell; 16 (main): Edd Westmacott/shot2bits.net, (inset upper): McPherson, (inset lower): Matt Farrow; 18: Joop Snijder jr./shutterstock; 19 (upper): Frank Baron, (lower): Jeff Banke/shutterstock; 20-23: Iren.k/shutterstock; 25 (main): Springoz/shutterstock, (inset upper): Anton Gvozdikov/shutterstock, (inset lower): Mark Winfrey/shutterstock; 26 (all): Mark Bennett; 29: Konstantin Mironov/shutterstock; 30-31 (main): peresanz/shutterstock; 33: Linda Nylind; 34: Linda Nylind; 35: Linda Nylind; 36 (all): Tom Pearson; 37 Tom Pearson; 38: Mike Evans; 39 (upper): ahlan/shutterstock, (lower): Mike Evans; 40: Phil Jones; 41 (both): Phil Jones; 42: Ben Rogers; 43: Ben Rogers; 46: Mark McNulty; 50: Ian Blacker; 54-55 (photo): Graeme Dawes/shutterstock, (illustration): Brett Wilkinson; 57 (both): Andy Boughflower/Ministry of Fun; 58 (main): Andy Boughflower/Ministry of Fun, (inset): Steve Razzetti; 59 (both): Rockness.co.uk; 60 (main & inset upper): Andy Boughflower/Ministry of Fun, (inset lower):

Published by Guardian Books 2009

2 4 6 8 10 9 7 5 3 1

First published in Great Britain in 2009 by
Guardian Books
90 York Way
London N1 9AG

www.guardianbooks.co.uk

A CIP catalogue record for this book is available from the British Library

ISBN 978-0852651261

Designed and typeset by Two Associates
Printed and bound in Great Britain
by Butler Tanner & Dennis